For Nigel, my dear husband, for all his support.

Also in memory of another special little dog.

Otto

'Your wings were ready, but my heart was not.'

Just Another Hound

© *copyright 2016*

Suzanne Cadwallader

The moral right of the author has been asserted.

All rights reserved.

No part of this publication may be reproduced, copied or transmitted by any means electronic, mechanical, photocopying or otherwise without the prior permission of the author.

First Edition

ISBN 978 1546894063

Disclaimer: Whereas this story is based on truth and anecdotal evidence, some assumptions have been made, names changed and characters invented to protect the identities of the people involved in rescuing these poor animals. Any resemblance to persons alive or dead is coincidental.

Author's note:

Cyprus is a beautiful island and holiday destination for many, but if you look behind the façade of the luxury hotels, apartments, restaurants and bars there is an ugly reality for many animals.

This book is dedicated to all the wonderful, compassionate people in Cyprus, who fight the unending fight to rescue, rehabilitate and rehome the countless, neglected, abandoned and abused dogs on the island.

It is also a tribute to the people worldwide who support their work with donations, fostering and adoptions.

With gratitude and heartfelt thanks for their work, all profits from the sale of this book will be shared between Rehoming Cyprus Pointers and Saving Pound Dogs Cyprus so that their work can continue.

It is my dream that this book will be translated into Greek and used, if possible, to help in some way, to raise awareness about animal welfare among the younger generation in Cyprus, so that one day, with the continued dedication of all involved, the many dogs in Cyprus needing rescuing now, will become just a few.

That would make Cyprus a true paradise.

For further information on the work of the rescue groups in Cyprus go to:
www.rehomingcypruspointers.co.uk
https://spdc.org.uk

JUST ANOTHER HOUND

Rescue Dog to Hero Dog

*This book has been a labour of love.
I hope you enjoy reading Hector's story.*

Chapter 1

Somewhere inland on the island of Cyprus.

The warmth of my mother and four siblings was a comfort and reassurance in the first two weeks of my life; my early recollections, by the time my eyes opened, were of time spent with them in a large wooden box in a huge barn. The box was generously filled with soft hay and once a day, a small kind lady, her hair tied away from her face and wearing a pretty summer dress and pinafore would come to the barn humming a little tune and bringing food to our mother. The lady smelled of coffee and freshly baked bread and she gently murmured to our mother.

'Good girl Adra, what a wonderful mama you are to your beautiful puppies.' Our mother would greet her with a wag of her tail and lick her hand. The large bowl of food which, to our tiny but highly sensitive noses, smelled delicious was soon devoured and the lady patted her and stroked her ears whilst humming her little tune.

Our mother would then get back into our box taking care not to tread on us and settle down to feed us. We would scrabble over each other and attach ourselves to one of her teats and take our fill of warm creamy milk after which, she would gently lick our tiny bodies to keep us clean and we would all snuggle up together secure and safe in our small, cozy world and sleep.

Every so often our beautiful mother would leave us to stretch her legs and come back a short while later, check us all, counting to make sure we were all present and correct, then take her place back in the box and once more, we would scramble over each other, competing for the best place next to her. She really was the loveliest mother, with her sleek black coat, rich tan muzzle and paws and the softest kindest brown eyes you could ever wish for.

By and by, two small dark haired children, a boy of about six with a slightly awkward gait, self-consciously hanging on to his mother's hand and a girl of three, who was chattering and giggling, came into the building with their mother. They were excited, laughing and smiling as they looked down at me and my brothers and sisters.

'Now children be very gentle, these pups are still very young and handling them too much may upset Adra and we wouldn't want her to reject her babies, would we?'

'We won't mama, we'll be careful, we promise.' They reassured her. Soon their chubby little hands were stroking us gently and telling us how sweet we all were. Slightly afraid at first, we soon relaxed and enjoyed the caresses and the attention from the children. 'Can we give them all names mama?' The children begged.

'Yes of course you can. 'Let Magda name the girls and you, Nicos can name the boys.' Taking it in turns, the little girl with her finger on her lips and her deep brown pigtails swinging, named my sisters Elina and Cora and the shy good natured Nicos gave my two brothers the names Manus and Apollo.
'But mama, there are five puppies so there's one more to name, what shall we call this one?' asked Nicos, 'You choose his name mama please! Go on, go on!'
'Yes, Yes! Mama your turn!' Magda echoed.

'Very well' she said. 'Then I will name him Theo after the very first dog I ever knew as a child, he was a very special dog and I just know this little pup will be very special too.'
'Theo, Theo, Theo!' the children chimed whilst Nicos held me high up above his head and skipped around the barn with little Magda dancing along behind him. They were a kind-hearted family who seemed to love our mother and her puppies. What happiness and joy there was in the barn that day.

Every afternoon the children were permitted into the barn to see us and as we all grew stronger, we were allowed to get out of the box and play with them and each other in the big barn. We pounced and jumped, chased our tails, played tug of war with bits of string and scampered around until we all fell, exhausted and happy back in the comfort of our box next to our doting mother.

Nicos would visit more and more frequently and seemed to take a particular shine to me and favoured me above the other pups; I too sensed a strong bond forming between us and looked forward to his visits. He would stroke my fur, kiss my nose, scrunch up old newspaper into balls, throw them and say, 'Fetch Theo!' I soon learned that what he wanted was for me to run after the ball of paper and bring it back to him and for that I would get a fuss and sometimes a tender morsel of meat.

Growing rapidly, we were by now, eating solid food and relying on our mother's milk less and less so Nicos spent as much time as he could with me, teaching me little tricks like sit, stay, come, give paw and roll over. His parents thought it was hilarious to see such a small puppy performing these tricks but he made learning fun and our bond grew greater still. He was my best friend, I was his and I adored him with all my heart.

One day the children's parents came into the barn to check on our progress. The father was a small, calm man with a wiry frame, glossy black hair and a neatly trimmed moustache across his top lip. 'They're a fine litter of pups Lena,' he said picking us up one by one, looking us over before placing us back in the box. 'A fine litter! We should get a good price for them and that will help out with things on the farm, there's so much expense at the moment we need every bit we can get. We need to get the mechanic in to fix the tractor, and the olive trees don't look very promising this year either. The weather has been too dry and hot.'

'Don't worry about the farm Vlassis,' she said quietly, placing her hand on his shoulder. 'Everything will work out fine, you'll see. We've been through hard times before and we're still here, aren't we?' She gave his arm a gentle squeeze and with a warm smile said, 'Come on, it's time for lunch, let's go and eat.'

One night when we were about six weeks old, there was a distant rumble of thunder and very soon a full-scale storm raged above us. The rain clattered onto the roof of the barn and poured in where the tiles of the roof were broken and missing. The wind howled and the doors of the barn blew open with a loud crash and as the torrent tore through the farm, we could hear it bringing down branches and fences outside. The loud noises didn't worry us one bit however, as we were safe and secure in the driest part of the barn cuddled up together as close as we could get, to the warm body of our adorable mother.

The next morning dawned; the wind and rain had subsided and everything was calm, the sunlight sparkling brightly through the small opening high above our heads in the barn. Apollo, the largest and bravest of us pups was feeling adventurous. The big wooden barn door, having been blown open in the storm, was still slightly ajar so he trotted confidently towards it, closely followed by me and Elina while Manos and Cora hung back with cautious curiosity but still keen to share this new adventure. Soon we were staring in bewilderment at the big, wide world beyond the barn.

The sun's lustre warmed us and the large farm yard was bathed in a clear white light. Our young eyes, up to now only used to the shade of the barn, blinked quickly, adjusting to the dazzling daylight. All of a sudden, there was the deafening rumbling sound of an engine and the ground seemed to shake beneath us. Before we knew what was happening, a huge tractor was upon us and we scattered in all directions, trying to avoid the wide, heavy wheels threatening to crush our little bodies in their wake.

The door to the farm house flew open and Nicos came running towards us closely followed by Magda.

'Theo! Manus! Cora! Elina! Apollo!' He shouted in alarm.

I turned just in time to see little Elina the smallest of us pups disappear in a cloud of dust, as the giant wheels bore down on us. The next moment, as if by some gentle gust of wind, I felt myself lifted up and carried away; it was Nicos who now cradled me his arms, whilst his sister Magda rushed forward and tenderly gathered up Elina's little body and ran back towards the house, crying.

'Mama, Mama…. help us…the puppy! Mama the puppy! Mama! Mama!'

As quickly as the cloud of earth and sand had risen, it faded away. Nicos held me to him, hugging me so tightly, I thought he would squeeze the very breath from my body.

'Thank the Lord you are safe Theo, what were you thinking? You must take care. There are too many dangers in this world for little puppies, you must stay in the barn with your mother until you are older where you will be safe.'

He hurried into the barn and placed me back into the box where my other siblings had retreated and were now cowered, shivering with fright and seeking comfort next to the familiar warmth and scent of our mother.
'There you go Theo, be a good boy and I'll be back as soon as I can.' Nicos ran out of the barn towards the house, from where I could still hear the sound of little Magda crying.

Soon afterwards, hearing digging and weeping outside, we all crept tentatively to the barn door and watched as Magda, Nicos and their mother plaintively laid a small bundle into a hole beneath the lemon tree, covered it with earth and laid stones over the top. As they hugged their mother and shed their tears I somehow knew that we would never see little Elina again.

Saddened and confused by the loss of our little sister the days past slowly but under the watchful gaze of Nicos, Magda and our mother we started to explore the world outside our barn door and to experience its dangers and delights, and my heart dared to be excited.

Chapter 2

By the time we were eight weeks old, we understood that we needed to be wary of the farm vehicles and were alert to approaching engine noises and what that meant. We grew acclimatized to loud noises made by the machinery but we found that playing on the land, around the house, was safe and that our humans were to be trusted and counted on for kindness and food.

We enjoyed running around the land noses to the ground; chasing rabbits and birds. It seemed instinctive to do so; part of our DNA Nicos said because we were very special hunting dogs called Greek hare hounds. I didn't mind or care what breed we were. I just knew I loved life and that this was our little paradise on earth and we delighted in our new-found freedom and happiness.

One day soon after, when Nicos was at school, we heard an engine sound we didn't recognize coming along the dusty lane, leading up to the farm. It came to a stuttering halt in the yard. We watched as a tall, middle aged man in overalls and heavy boots strode deliberately up to the house and hammered on the door.

Feeling a little suspicious of this loud brash character, we all hid under the old table in the garden and peered out with baited breath. Soon Vlassis, the children's father, came to the door. He was obviously just in the middle of eating, as he still had a big cloth tied around his neck, which was stained with tomato sauce. Gesturing towards the garden he walked down the path with the scruffy man to where we were all hiding.

'Come on pups.' He said encouragingly, tempting us out with a tasty tit bit. As usual, confident Apollo was first out and the man picked him up, turning him this way and that, examining him carefully. His hands looked rough, ingrained with dirt and smelt of olives and grapes.
Vlassis began. 'He's certainly the pick of the litter Georgios, a fine example of a Greek hare hound. The children call him Apollo and he'll make a splendid hunter and great addition to your pack.'
'How is he around gunshot? Is he gun-shy?' The man enquired.

'No not at all Georgios, all the pups here are used to gun shots, you know well what a problem we have with the wild rabbits around here, so I'm always having to cull a few with my old rifle. No, he's a grand confident pup and will be a courageous hound when he's fully grown.'

'Well, as long as he can do the job, that's all I care about. He's just another hound at the end of the day and hounds need to know their place and earn their keep or they're no use. I'm not one for putting good money after bad or feeding a hound that doesn't know its place. I'll take him and see how he does. I can't say fairer than that.'

'Well, I was hoping for a good price Georgios, he's the strongest pup of the bunch and you know what a smashing lot the last litter were. You know how well we raise our pups here. We're not like a lot of breeders who keep the bitch tied up outside with no shelter and virtually having to fend for herself. No, we're not like that here. The mother has been kept in the barn, fed on good food and the pups are strong and healthy.'

'As I said, he's just another hound,' Giorgios replied. 'This is what I'm offering,' he said, holding out a few notes of money, 'take it or leave it, there's plenty of other pups around, why your neighbour down the hill has six that'll be ready next week. No, that's what I'm offering so it's up to you Vlassis. Times are hard and getting harder I reckon.'

I could sense Vlassis was disappointed but he took the money offered and they shook hands. Giorgios took Apollo under his arm and strode purposefully back to his truck. Putting Apollo on the back seat, he started the engine and drove off.

What this meant, we didn't know or understand. All we knew was that another of our siblings had gone and the children cried when they were told. Nicos came into the barn with dewy eyes and collected me up in his young arms, holding me to him, as if I was the most precious thing in the world.

'Oh, Theo I don't know what I would do without you boy, I pray every night that papa will let you stay here with me. I know we need the money but to me you are worth much more than money. I wish I was a millionaire and then I could buy mama and papa a brand-new tractor for the farm and you, Cora and Manus could stay here forever and we would all be so happy!' I lifted my head and licked his little nose.

Although we all missed our bigger, bolder brother, for a few more days at least, we were distracted by playing around the grounds with Nicos and Magda. We rested in the shade of the olive groves when the heat of the sun became too hot to bear, and at night slept peacefully in the comfort of the barn with our mother.

Our idyll was not to last long however and soon, two more trucks swept into the yard, men got out, examined us pups and before I knew it Cora and Manus were bought, money exchanged and the children wept again as we watched the pups disappearing into trucks down the dusty track, away from the farm, to a place we knew not where.

I felt abandoned; whimpering for my lost brothers and sister. My soft-hearted mother soothed me and the children tried hard to comfort me with cuddles and games, amusing me with chase and fetch and gradually, I thought less and less about my missing siblings. Over the next few weeks, I grew into a smaller but none the less handsome image of my mother and became Nicos's little shadow. I took to following him everywhere and our lives became as one, as our bond grew stronger still.

Every weekday morning, he would leave for school with his little back pack and I would trot alongside him, listening to his boyish dreams. Once at the school, I would hide and drowse beneath the old wooden bench under a lemon tree. There, a short distance away from the school gate, I waited until the bell rang when I knew Nicos would come running out to hug me and take me home.

Little Magda was not yet old enough to go to school but she would always be at the farm gate waiting for us to come home. She would always have a tasty treat ready and covered my head with tender little kisses. Then the children would feed me, brush me and bathe me to keep me free of fleas and ticks and we would play in the shade of the olive grove. I loved those children so much, my heart seemed to swell up with pride whenever I was near them.

One day the school bell rang, signalling the end of lessons for the day. All the children came running out of school, some mounted bikes to cycle home, a few were met by parents in cars or trucks, but most of the children ran or walked home, laughing and chatting with each other as they went.

I sat patiently waiting for Nicos, scanning each child's face hoping to see him emerge from the school building. He was late and I began to worry. After a while, when all the others had gone, Nicos finally and warily put his head around the door as if expecting some hidden danger but seeing only me, ran as fast as his little legs would carry him and hugged me close to his chest.

'Theo, good boy for waiting, sorry I'm so late. It's been one of those days!'

I could sense Nicos was sad and his sweet face had tear stains running down his cheeks. Somebody or something had upset my boy. I licked his face tenderly, trying to wash away his pain and he kissed me on my nose.
'Come on boy, let's go home.'
He skipped along and I ran with him. Soon we were at the edge of the village, where houses were replaced by olive groves and ramshackle farm buildings.

'Hey, Nicos!! You little squirt! Got my money eh? You're overdue with this week's payment and why have you got that pathetic dog eh? Don't you know he's just a hound, a hunting dog? No good for anything else. They're not pets you idiot, they're just stupid hounds. On top of that he's black which you know is bad luck and it's definitely bad luck for you today!… We're going to give you a good going over! We'll teach you not to forget our money and then we'll kick your dog as well for good measure!'

It was two boys, bigger than Nicos and probably a year or so older, who had lain in wait to ambush him. Nicos simultaneously glanced round to see who it was, dropped his school bag and started running, as if his life depended on it, along the dirt track with me in hot pursuit. The bigger boys were faster and stronger and were quickly gaining ground.

'Coward! Give us your money or stand and fight!' They yelled whilst almost upon him.

I didn't know why or what primeval instinct took over but I just realised that I had to do something.

As we came to the narrow path that we used as a short cut between the old stone walls, I span around to face the fast approaching bullies. Nicos, sensing my intentions, just kept running.

I rose up on my hind legs and barked with all my might. The bark of an adolescent hare hound is not as impressive as a fully grown adult dog but it certainly comes close and the boys stopped dead in their tracks. They knew they couldn't get past without risking a bite to their legs and the high walls either side of the path, cut off any alternative route. I growled and snarled and bared my teeth menacingly, warning them off.

Glancing around, I was most relieved to see that Nicos had made good headway, so, giving one final bark, as loud as I could muster, I turned tail and chased after him.

By the time we arrived at the farm house, we were both panting hard and dying of thirst. His kind mother gave us both a drink and sat him down and listened compassionately as he told her, through his tears, about the bullies; how they had been extorting money from some of children including him and how they'd been picking on him and hitting him when he didn't have 'the protection money'.

All I could do was put my head in his lap and try to console him.

'Nicos my sweet boy, why didn't you tell me or your father what was going on or go to your teacher?'

'I didn't want to worry you mama. I know you and papa are concerned about things on the farm and I thought I could deal with it by myself. I'm sorry. If it hadn't been for Theo, I would have been well and truly beaten up today. I promise if there's any other trouble, I will tell you.'

'You know you can always tell your parents anything Nicos. We love you and the last thing we want is for you to be unhappy.' She hugged her son to her and kissed the top of his young head.

The next day the children's mother accompanied us to school. I waited in my usual place and shortly afterwards, she came out smiling, patted my dark sleek head, caressed my long soft ears and murmured.
'Good lad Theo, I knew you were a special dog.' Then she set off back to the farm humming her special little tune.

As far as I know those bullies never bothered Nicos or the other children again and my heart felt proud.

Chapter 3

The oppressive, hot, languorous days of the Cypriot summer were drawing in and an unfamiliar breeze swept in over the island and our small farm. There had been very little rain and the weather unusually hot and the olive harvest was poor. I could tell that the children's parents were under pressure and anxious about things. Often, I would hear raised voices and their father Vlassis would storm out, slam the door and take himself off, down the lane, coming back late into the night smelling very strongly of wine or beer.

Nicos and Magda seemed somehow subdued, their laughter less spontaneous and the food they brought to me and my mother became less frequent. Nicos would still hold me close and sometimes brought me some extra bread soaked in milk or olive oil, which I took from him gently, careful not to hurt his small hand with its precious offering. He knew I was still growing and needed nutritious meals but I soon understood that this bread was coming from his own plate and I refused to accept it, although I was terribly hungry.

'Theo,' he wept. 'Papa says we can't afford to keep two dogs here anymore and you must be sold because he can breed more puppies from Adra. What's to be done boy?'

I gently nuzzled into his little neck taking in the comforting and familiar scent of his slight frame. Then, looking straight into his tearful hazel eyes, I tried to communicate to him that it would be ok and he wasn't to worry, but all that came out was a pitiful little whimper as he cried into my fur.

Soon afterwards, in the early evening, another strange truck rumbled up the track to the farm. Money quickly changed hands and I was roughly gathered up and pushed onto the back seat of an old truck by a fat old man smelling of stale tobacco and rancid oil mingled with the stench of guns and ammunition.

He slammed the door and took the wheel when, suddenly, Nicos came rushing out of the house. The truck set off. Alarmed at being separated from Nicos, I jumped up, desperately trying to look out of the back window but it was covered in grime and filth. Disconsolate, all I could do was to listen to the chugging of the old truck and a small boy's voice screaming.

'Theo! Theo! No Papa no! Theo! Theo!'

As the distraught little voice faded and was overtaken by the growl of the diesel engine, all I felt was emptiness and my heart wept.

Chapter 4

The journey was a long and decidedly uncomfortable one. The truck was old and full of rubbish, so there was nowhere to sit or lie down and I was forced to stand all the way. Whenever we went over a pothole, my head bumped into the roof and I was thrown forward several times, bashing into the back of the front seats.

'Stand still dog!' Commanded the smelly old man.

That was impossible and although the weather at that time of year was beginning to cool down, the inside of the truck smelled sweaty and sour. By the time we stopped I felt parched, ravenously hungry and exhausted.

The back door was flung open and the old man slipped a rope leash around my neck. 'Out you get dog…hurry up!' He pulled on the rope which tightened around my neck and I fell out awkwardly, landing on the stony ground, head first.

'Stupid animal!' He snapped, yanking hard on the rope. I'd never been used to being on a leash before. I'd always just followed Nicos wherever he wanted to go, so this was all new and unsettling.

The smelly old man dragged me roughly across the uneven ground, almost choking me with the rope. My paws scraped along the sharp, jagged stones as we went, making them bleed.
Despite the fading light, I saw a small cramped cage with three other hunting dogs inside; a female black and white pointer and slightly bigger brown and white male pointer and another large adult male hare hound like myself. Their heads and tails were down and they looked dejected and forlorn. This was not going to be a nice life and I longed for the comfort and security of my home and Nicos's tender care.

The bulging, grimy old man pushed me into the cage, removing the rope from my neck, banged the door shut, rammed home the lock and shuffled off towards a small stone house further up the track, where a single light glimmered in the fast approaching gloom.

Only ever having known the love and companionship of my brothers and sisters I wasn't accustomed to meeting new dogs at such close quarters and nervously sidled around the edge of the cage, hoping that they would be friendly but also seeking some water to quench my thirst.

The other dogs approached me and the male pointer lifted his head inhaling my scent, checking me out. The other two followed suit, and happy I wasn't a threat, they came closer and we greeted each other in the time honoured canine way.

Relieved that my new acquaintances weren't going to attack me, I relaxed a little and took my fill from an old bucket of green, fetid, muddy water that I'd spotted. No food though, I observed. Maybe the old man would feed us tomorrow?

Later, the old man came out of the house and fired his rifle into the air above the cage. I stayed still, not knowing what was coming next.

'At least you're not gun shy, dog. That's one thing going for you.' He muttered ruefully and went back inside.

Tomorrow came; still no food was provided and my hunger was growing.

Three days later, having had no food at all and living in our own mess, we were jolted awake very early as the malodorous old man clattered a metal rod against the side of the cage.

'Up dogs! Get up you lazy louts! Let's be having you!'

He came into the cage, tied ropes around each of our necks and tugged us roughly out to another bigger truck. This time I didn't resist but followed the rest of the dogs: They seemed to know the routine and anyway it spared my sore paws any further trauma on the sharp stones. It appeared that none of us were to be given names, we were just dogs, pieces of property; just hounds, there to do a job.

After about half an hour's bumpy ride into the hills, we came to an abrupt halt at the end of a rough dirt track in a small clearing in the woods, miles from anywhere.

'Out dogs! Out now!' He grunted. 'Come on!'

I followed the others, jumping smartly out of the truck. The old man, holding a rifle under his arm, yelled.

'Away dogs! Away!'

The other three dogs shot off at full pelt, barking and baying into the woods. I followed, instinctively, hoping to learn what all this was about. In an instant, a large buck rabbit darted out from the undergrowth right across our path. The pack gave chase and corralled the prey into a v shape and back towards the old man where he stood, rifle at the ready.

It was over in a flash. The shot was fired and the rabbit knocked off its feet, dead.

Smelling the blood and as ravenous as I was, I just grabbed the dead corpse.

'Here dog! Bring!' The old man hollered.

I hesitated. I was starving and didn't want to relinquish this fresh meat.

'Here! Bring!' He echoed.

What was I to do? I bit into the juicy, flavoursome flesh of the rabbit carcass and retreated into the undergrowth to eat the first decent meal I'd had in days.

'Bad dog!' He yelled as he hit my muzzle with the butt of his rifle, forcing me to drop my meal. I'd been so absorbed in eating, that I hadn't even noticed the old man approaching and the other three dogs observing me, from a distance, with my feast.

'Thieving hound! Get back into the truck now!'

My nose was bleeding from the sharp crack to my jaw and feeling a little dazed I was hauled back to the truck and locked in.

I could still hear the other dogs as they went back to work and several shots later, the truck door opened and the other three dogs bundled in. The old man clambered on to his seat and drove back to the small holding, locked us back into the cage and gathering up his kill from the truck, he shambled up to the house, slamming the door.

Later that evening the old man came down to the cage with a large bowl of slops, bits of bread, bones and some sort of grain. I could hardly contain my excitement in anticipation of at last getting fed but instead, the flabby old man placed the bowl on top of the cage, tied the rope around my neck and tethered it tightly to the door frame. He dropped the bowl of food onto the floor for the other three dogs, who ate hungrily.

Unable to reach the food, I just had to watch and whine in self- pity.

After the others had finished their meal, the vile old man untied me and led me up towards the house.

I first smelt, then saw the dead rabbit lying invitingly on the ground. Joy! I was getting a meal! He let the rope length out so that I could grab the moist meat.

Agony! My whole body leaped up and crashed down with the searing pain that shot through my mouth.

'That'll teach you to steal my kill, you filthy mutt!' He sneered.

He'd placed electrodes inside the meat, which had given me a huge electric shock, as soon as I touched it.

'Still hungry dog?' He said contemptuously 'No, I thought not!'

I spent the next three days recovering from this callous act, lying on my side in the cold hard and comfortless cage, my mouth burnt and blistered.

I heard and smelt the older male pointer occasionally approach to sniff me but I was in too much pain to even lift my head and look at him.

The old man come in to sluice the cage of faeces and urine but he just ignored me. He just didn't care.

Eventually, I fell to sleep and dreamt of my boy hugging and kissing me.

When I awoke, my heart felt discarded and forlorn.

Chapter 5

After three days, it was time to go hunting again even though my mouth was still racked with pain from the electrical burns and my stomach empty: We were once more bundled into the truck and taken up the hill to the clearing:

'Out!' the old man commanded.

We all obeyed, running off to round up a few rabbits, hares and birds for the old man to shoot. He enjoyed a good kill that day, and we at least got a well-deserved meal. Despite this we were still constantly hungry and our skin irritated by the fleas and ticks that lived on our bodies, feeding from our blood.

The next day the old man hosed down our cage which was covered with excrement. He only did it once a week if we were lucky and we would struggle to find a remotely clean spot to lie amid the stench: plagued by the swarms of flies that the filth attracted.

A young man of about twenty and a slightly slimmer version of the old man, arrived at the house on foot with a young, playful female Jura hound puppy of about four or five months old. She was a beautiful chestnut colour, with the longest silkiest ears I'd ever seen.

'Hey! Hi, Grandad I'm here as promised. I've brought the pup so she can start her training.'

The old man put down the hose, turned off the tap and took hold of the pup as if appraising her fitness.

'How is she round gunshot Darius?' He asked the lad.

'I'm not sure Grandad, I don't think she's heard any yet, but I'm sure she'll be fine.'

'Well, we can make sure she is easy enough.' The old man rasped.

'Just wait here, I'll be back in a minute.'

The young lad came towards our cage. 'Hi you lot! Have you been good?'
Noticing me he said, 'You're a new fella, what a handsome lad you are.' Putting his hand through the cage he stroked my dark ears. 'Good boy!' he said.

Just now, the old man reappeared holding his rifle, a hammer and a few nails.
'Right, just put her down while I fire the gun.' He said.

The poor pup bolted as soon as she heard the shot. 'That's no-good Darius! We can't have dogs running around everywhere when the gun's fired. Bring her here and hold her firmly while I nail her ears down.'

'Are you sure this is ok Grandad? It seems a bit brutal.'
'Don't be soft lad. Of course it's ok. I've always done it to all the gun-shy dogs I've had. It teaches them to stay still when they hear the gun. It's the old way and the only way!'

Despite looking uncertain, Darius complied and helped the old man by holding the poor pup down while his grandfather hammered two nails through her beautiful shiny ears, into the ground. She screamed and squealed and bled. Then, as she writhed in terror and pain, he fired the gun over her head again and again until she became silent and still.

Darius stood, flinching at each shot but allowed the unspeakable cruelty to continue while we other dogs looked on in horror and disgust.

The young pup trembled and shook as they ripped the nails out of her ears, leaving bleeding holes behind.
Darius picked her up, wiping the blood away and tried to comfort the little soul.

'There, there little one. It's ok.' He whispered.

His grandfather was scathing: 'Don't fuss over her lad, she needs toughening up. She's just a hound for god's sake! They don't need fussing, just firm discipline!'

Darius pushed the pup into the cage with us, a tear drop in his eye. His heart wasn't yet as hard as his grandfather's but over time, I could sense that would change and that he would become like him: Cruel and callous.

As he left, we all surrounded the little pup to comfort and protect her from the heartless world she now inhabited, while she cried and whimpered through her fear and pain.

Weeks passed and the pup grew. Sooner than expected, the winter weather was upon us and icy winds rattled through the cage, which offered little respite from the icy blasts. At least after each hunt, we were rewarded with a bowl of food. That still only meant one decent meal every three to four days. How could we survive and work on so little sustenance?

My coat lost its shine and we all felt miserable. The young pup was still growing and needed more food but it was particularly severe on the big male pointer who had been unstintingly kind to me. You could see in him, what remained of a once magnificent, athletic dog but even now, at the age of only three or four, he was starting to slow down and look old. This hard life was taking its toll. He was stiff jointed after every hunt and the pup and I would huddle up next to him, trying to ease his discomfort with the heat from our own bodies.

One Sunday in late January the weather was particularly miserable; it had rained all night and a bitter wind had left patches of ice in our cage and on the ground outside. Loaded once more into the truck, the old man headed up towards his favourite hunting ground in the hills. As the truck chugged up the rough track, the weather deteriorated first to sleet and then to snow. By the time we reached our normal clearing, there were at least two or three inches on the ground and the wind was threatening to whip up a real blizzard.

Despite the adverse conditions, we were dragged out of the truck and given the command to hunt. The old man stood shivering, despite several layers of clothes, hugging his rifle.

Our pack set out baying and barking through the snow-covered undergrowth and trees, hoping to flush out a rabbit or two. We knew that without a decent kill the old man wouldn't give us much to eat that night, so it was imperative that we gave him what he wanted.

The thick layer of snow disguised the terrain under our paws but still we ran as quickly as we could to and fro; working hard and ploughing our way through the heavily laden bushes, leaving clouds of white dust behind us as we went.

More than a little disorientated, I lost sight of the rest of the pack through the driving snow. Suddenly I heard a sickening yelp come from one of the other dogs, followed soon after by a shout from the old man, calling us back to the truck.

I turned to sniff the air, trying to locate the other dogs and as I followed it, I came upon my friend, the big brown and white pointer, lying awkwardly in the freezing snow.

His leg was twisted out of shape beneath him and he looked in a bad way. He'd misjudged the ground and not being able to see clearly, he'd caught his foot in a rabbit hole, obscured by the thick layer of snow. As I approached, he whined pitifully and tried to lift himself up but stumbled, unable to support himself and fell back once again, whimpering in pain. Licking his head gently, I tried to encourage him to try once more but it was no use, his leg was so badly broken that the old dog needed help that I couldn't provide.

I stayed with him and started barking as loudly as I could, hoping that the old man would find us and rescue my friend. Eventually, I saw his shuffling figure emerge through the curtain of white, while we shivered in the sub-zero temperature. At last help was at hand!

I wagged my tail enthusiastically, pleased to see him but the hateful old man just stood, looking down at the big dog impassively and shook his head.

'No use to me now dog,' he muttered under his breath, 'no use at all.'

Without hesitation, he lifted his rifle and shot the poor dog through the head, turned, without even a backward glance and fought his way through the freezing snow to the truck.

Stunned at what I had just witnessed, I didn't know what to do.

The old man called me again and again. 'Dog, here! Come here!' I remained immobilized by shock at my old companion's cruel death.

Soon afterwards, I heard the truck's engine start up and rumble away with a muffled groan down the snowy track.

I turned back towards the lifeless body of the once noble pointer. His corpse was now almost covered in snow, save for a large patch of red seeping from his poor head, across the blanket of white. I realised that there was nothing more that could help the old hunter now and giving him a final mournful lick, my heart grieved.

Chapter 6

What was I to do? Alone, freezing and half-starved, I fought my way through the snow to an old hollow tree trunk, lying on the ground. Acutely aware of my predicament, I crawled inside the trunk and waited for the snow storm to pass.

I must have fallen to sleep for, when I opened my eyes, the snow had abated and the sun was rising, reflecting the shimmering light on the crystalline icicles, creating a magical winter wonderland. I crept from my hiding place and shook myself awake. Looking around and sniffing the icy air, I tentatively made my way down the hillside and away from the horrors of the day before.

The last place I wanted to be was back with the old man. I couldn't and wouldn't go back to him. He had shattered my faith in humankind.

As I struggled down the hill the snow gradually gave way to slush and icy puddles. In the far distance, I could just make out a small holding in the stony dip of the valley. Reaching the perimeter of the land, I approached with care.

Some deliciously tantalizing aromas emanated from the small house, which made my hunger pangs even more acute. Sniffing and snuffling around, I suddenly came across a small group of hens pecking around for seeds and worms in the hard ground. Never having killed anything before, I really didn't know what to do, but my hunger was unbearable and coupled with instinct and impulse, I just hurtled headlong into the flock!

The chickens scattered, clucking and screeching with fear. The cacophonous commotion disturbed the owner, a youngish man with dark unruly hair and unkempt beard, who rushed out of the house to investigate. Seeing me floundering around in the middle of the startled hens with a mouthful of brown feathers incensed him. Picking up a large stone, he hurled it at me.

'Get out of here you thieving hound!' He yelled, turning back to the house to retrieve a rifle from behind the door, he took aim and fired!

The bullet whistled passed my head!

That was enough to convince me that I wasn't welcome there and that my life was in jeopardy. Retreating as fast as I could through the mud, I felt bitter disappointment; all I had to show for my endeavours was a mouthful of feathers and I was still as hungry as ever.

With increased vigilance, I followed the winding dirt track from the house to what I hoped would be some civilization and possibly food. I was ravenous and finding myself so abandoned, felt fearful and apprehensive.

My early memories had taught me that people and particularly children were usually generous and kind, but these beliefs had been seriously dented by recent events. I'd always been a well behaved and obedient dog, so why wouldn't anyone help me?

I could only follow my nose and ploughed on.

Eventually I came across a small village. It was still raining; bitterly cold and hunger pangs were gnawing away inside me. I was so very desperate for food.

Spotting a discarded bin bag at the side of the road, I clawed my way through the plastic in the hope of finding some leftovers but all I found were empty foil containers and a moldy piece of bread.
It smelt and tasted awful but I ate it anyway but it wasn't enough to satisfy my hunger.

In such despair, I was reduced to roaming around the village, scavenging for scraps of anything remotely edible. I slept anywhere I could to hide away from the villagers who chased me away, kicked me and hit me with anything they had to hand.

'Get away, you filthy black dog! Off with you. Shoo!'

Driven by hunger and fearful for my safety I left that village and followed the road ahead. By now I was feeling weak and exhausted: All I'd had to eat was a few chicken bones and water from filthy puddles. Helpless and hopeless, desperation set in.

Eventually, as I rounded a sharp bend in the road, I could just make out the roof tops of a few houses at the edge of a town with smoke rising from their chimneys.

What I would give for a meal and a warm safe place to sleep. Heaven. The nearer I got, the wonderful smell of roasting meat permeated the air and my stomach lurched at the prospect of a meal! Perhaps I would have better luck here?

The source of this delicious aroma was a small taverna on the edge of the town. Being winter, the doors and windows were shut and steamed up with condensation. Jumping up, I placed my front paws on the window ledge in the hope of getting a better view and a glimpse of the cooked meat.

Through the misty glass, I could just make out a family of five, two adults and three children sitting around a table covered with a gingham tablecloth. In front of them a candle, a bottle of wine, a jug of water, crusty bread and plates of luscious lamb casserole. My mouth salivated and drooled at the sight of this rich feast and I longed for just one small mouthful of the scrumptious stew.

Suddenly, I heard somebody approaching. Scared of another beating I jumped down and quickly took refuge behind some dustbins at the back of the taverna. Peeking out cautiously, I saw a frail young girl of perhaps fifteen or sixteen years old. She looked vulnerable and was woefully thin. Her long dark hair hung around her pale face like curtains and she was shivering from the cold. She didn't have a coat and just wore flimsy summer sandals on her little feet. As she made her way towards the back door, I tried to slip further behind the bins to conceal my presence.

Crash! A crate of empty wine bottles went flying!

'Who's there?' she called out, startled.

In an instant, a large, balding, overweight man, wearing a grubby cooking apron, barged out through the back door. His shirt sleeves were rolled up to reveal dark inky tattoos on his forearms.

'Stella, is that you making that noise? Not only are you late but you're disturbing our customers, stupid girl! Get this mess cleaned up now and then get inside, there's work to be done! Quick!' He banged the door behind him and was gone.

Stella started to retrieve the bottles and broken glass, placing the undamaged ones back into the crate. In the failing light, still concealed behind the bins, I watched her closely and winced for her when she accidentally cut her finger on a shard of glass. She sucked on it to stem the flow of blood as she knelt down, trying to find every last piece with her other hand.

Bit by bit she was edging nearer and nearer to my hiding place and without making a break for it and risking another beating, all I could do was stay put, in the hope she wouldn't find me. Her delicate fingers scrabbled around in her search of the fragments of glass and gradually crept towards me in the dusk. Soon they were within a few centimetres of my paws and then, she found fur.

'Oh, good grief, what's that!' She exclaimed, quickly withdrawing her hand and pulling back in alarm.

I crept out sheepishly from my dark corner. Still on her hands and knees, our eyes met instantly in the shadows. I wagged my tail slowly, warily and whimpered.

'Oh, you poor dog,' she whispered, glancing around her furtively, afraid to attract any attention from inside the taverna or from other customers arriving or leaving. She held out her small, red, chapped hand and I gently sniffed it, giving it a tentative little lick with my tongue.

'Good dog…don't be frightened little fella.' She stroked my head soothingly, sensing my apprehension as her hand moved down to my sides. 'You poor thing, you're just skin and bone. You must be starving. Good boy, stay there. I promise I will bring you something to eat later but you'll have to be patient and wait.'

She softly patted my head and I slid back into my hiding place. I somehow knew that I could trust this young girl with the sad eyes.

The diners in the taverna were quite rowdy that night and at some point, they sang a birthday song to one of the children, which was followed by enthusiastic clapping and cheering.
 Slowly, after eating their fill, they left and the place fell quiet except for the sounds emanating from the kitchen of pots and pans being washed, dried and put away.

Presently, I heard the sound of the front door being locked and a man's irritated voice shouting:

'Stella, finish up here, mop the floor in the taverna and the kitchen before you go. Don't forget to lock the back door and turn off the lights! I'm going home to bed!'

The man came out, slammed the back door, stopped to light a cigarette, adjusted his coat against the weather, got into his car and drove off.
Still, I didn't move, but crouched down between the bins waiting.

Eventually my patience was rewarded and Stella put her head around the door, checking that the coast was clear and emerged carrying a large, appetizing bowl of warm scraps.

'Here we are boy, come here.' She placed the bowl on the ground by the door but despite my desperate hunger, I held back. Recollections of those terrible electrodes burning my mouth were a stark reminder of the need for caution.

'It's ok. Eat it boy.' She urged, pushing the bowl towards me. This time I didn't need further encouragement and greedily wolfed down the wonderful meal. It may have been just leftovers but to me it was ambrosia, the delicious food of the gods!

Stella stood by in silence until I'd finished and then proffered another bowl and at last I could quench my thirst with the first fresh, clean water I'd had in ages.

'What am I going to do with you boy?' She said sympathetically. I looked up into her doleful childlike face and wagged my tail.

'Woof!' I barked, trying to say thank you.

'You'll have to stop that barking for a start,' she whispered, 'you'll need to be silent and invisible if I'm going to keep you away from Uncle Stephan, not to mention the awful dog catchers and the municipal dog pound! Follow me boy, come on.'

She patted the side of her leg and I immediately took my place by her side and followed my sweet, newly acquired best friend. At the back of the building, set a little distance apart, was a rickety hut which served as a wood store, supplying the heating in the taverna during the winter months.

'You can sleep in here tonight boy, there's some old hessian sacks to lie on and at least it's out of the wind and rain.' She cleared a small space and I settled down on the make shift bedding, between the wood piles and watched as Stella filled a basket with heavy logs and hauled it slowly and laboriously to the back door, in readiness for the next day. Collecting up the two bowls I'd used, she went back inside to finish her work. It must have been almost midnight when she returned, patted my head gently and breathed, 'Good night boy, you stay here, sweet dreams, see you tomorrow.'

I watched as she hurried away. Glancing back just once, she clutched her thin cardigan to her, in a vain attempt to keep the wind and rain from soaking her frail body. I settled down in the relative luxury of a dry, sheltered bed and my heart felt grateful.

Chapter 7

These halcyon days lasted for a few weeks, me, hiding in the wood shed by day and being fed and tended by the sweet girl with the sad eyes at night. She would feed me and groom me, freeing me of the ticks and fleas that had infested my body whilst living on the streets and nursing me back to health. My ribs stopped showing through my fur once more and my sleek, black coat returned.

After she'd gone home each night, I would occasionally go for a short walk to stretch my legs in the relative concealment of the dark chilly nights. I steered clear of human contact but often encountered other abandoned dogs, scavenging around for a crumb or crust to salve their aching hunger and witnessed the intolerance of the residents and business owners in the village. They chased the starving dogs away, kicking them and throwing stones at them; even setting down poisoned meat for them, so that they would die a slow agonizing death, in some dreadful ditch without a word of comfort or hope.

Grateful for what I had back at the taverna, I would retreat to the wood store and sleep contentedly until Stella's next visit.

The first hint of spring came early and a new warmth brought the music of bird song and buds on the vines and trees. Longer days of course meant shorter nights and soon gentle Stella was bringing food to me before it was completely dark. She'd also given me a name shortly after we'd met.

'I can't have a dog without a name,' she'd announced, 'I shall call you Alexis!' So, Alexis became my new name and I felt loved once more.

I had always felt that Stella's fragility was tinged with a deep unhappiness and there was an air of resignation about her. Shouting and banging in the kitchen after the taverna closed was a regular occurrence and I would hear Stephan yelling at her repeatedly, once the customers had left.

Later on, when she brought my food, I would sometimes detect a bruise or welt on her arms and tear stains on her dear face. However, she always beamed her warm, loving smile whenever she saw me and, because of that, I was reassured that she was alright and would relax and enjoy her company, caresses and hugs.

We were two of a kind Stella and I, both lost souls united in love and our friendship was unshakeable.

Naturally, the warmer weather meant that the back door to the kitchen was wedged open to let the heat and humidity from all the cooking escape. The wonderful aroma of the delectable dishes on the menu were like heaven to my highly sensitive nose and I felt lucky to be able to sample them when Stella brought me the leftovers, after everyone else had gone.

One night, as I lay quietly concealed in the wood shed, I heard a loud crash as a plate or glass hit the floor.

'Stupid little cow! These plates cost money you know! I don't buy them for you to smash on the floor, do I? Well? Do I?' Hollered the irascible Stephan.

'No uncle, I'm sorry, I'm sorry! I'll pay for the damage.' Stella cried.

'Pay! What with? I don't pay you enough for that! No, I'll just teach you a lesson on how to be more careful with things that don't belong to you, you little witch!'

Fearful for my friend I stole stealthily from my hiding place and watched the unfolding drama through the open door of the starkly lit kitchen. Alarmed, I saw that Stephan had hold of Stella by her hair, which he followed by a swift punch to her stomach.

She cried out in pain. 'Please uncle, No! Please don't! Please!'
Still pulling at her hair, he raised his arm to punch her again.

I pounced!

'Aahhg!' He bawled as I leapt up and seized his wrist in my jaws, biting down as hard as I could!

'Aahhg! Aahhg!'

Stella was sobbing. 'No Alexis! Let him go! Stop it!'

I released my grip but stood, teeth bared, between Stella and her uncle.

'Almighty God!' He blasphemed 'Look what that damn dog has done! Where did he come from? I'm bleeding to death! Don't just stand there! Do something! Do something!'

Feeling empowered, Stella regained her composure and countered.

'You're not bleeding to death at all Stephan. You're just a coward and bully who picks on those weaker than you. Now, at last, you've got what you deserve!'

'Get out Stella! Get out! Before I kill you! And don't dare come back. You're fired!' He bellowed as he rushed to the sink to rinse his wounded arm under the tap.

'That damned dog could have rabies for all I know! God, it hurts like hell!'

Stella, as a last act of kindness, threw him a tea towel to wrap his arm in and marched through the door, closely followed by me; a newly nourished, loved and magnificent black and tan dog and my heart felt courageous.

Chapter 8

The block of flats where Stella lived were grey and unwelcoming. Being on the other side of the town they seemed poor and ill kept compared to the buildings on the more upmarket side of town, where Stephan's taverna was situated. There was a tobacconist, seedy bar, frequented by drunks and a cheap pizza takeaway on the ground floor with the residential apartments on the next three levels.

As we entered the building, we saw an old man in a corner, curled up on some old cardboard. He was sleeping with a tattered blanket covering his body and an empty beer bottle by his side. The elevator was out of order, so we had to climb the two flights of grimy, littered stairs which stank of unwashed bodies and urine.

'Be very quiet boy, we mustn't let on that you're here, no pets allowed you see.' Stella whispered, unlocking the apartment door.

There was a small table lamp in the corner of the sparsely furnished sitting room which contained a small kitchen area and to the right, another door slightly ajar with a dim yellow light beyond.

'Mama are you awake?' She murmured as she quietly pushed the door open a little further.

'Yes Stella, I was worried, are you ok?' A hoarse voice answered.

Stella signalled for me to wait and she went in. I sensed that this was a time for them to be alone but I listened attentively as Stella poured out the story of how her uncle had been emotionally and physically abusing her for three years.

As she related the unbearable details, she wept and her mother wept with her. Peeking through the door I could see mother and child holding each other as if they couldn't bear to be parted. Stella's mother's eyes were brimming with tears and she kept asking why she'd kept this secret for so long, then weeping and saying how sorry she was, that it was her fault, how she should have realised what was going on and what a bad mother she'd been.

'No mama, you are a wonderful mother; I love you with all my heart. Don't blame yourself. Uncle Stephan is the guilty one. I'm so sorry I didn't tell you before but you're so poorly and I didn't want to worry you. We've needed the money to make ends meet since papa left us and Stephan kept telling me that if I left the taverna he'd make sure I wouldn't find work anywhere else. He told me so many times how stupid I was well, I began to believe him too.'

'My sweet girl, no amount of money is worth putting up with that sort of abuse. My precious child, I'm your mother. You can tell me anything. I know my condition is deteriorating but whatever happens, we'll survive. You'll get another job despite what Stephan says because you're hardworking, honest and trustworthy. If he tries to sully your name, we'll report him to the authorities for what he's done and they'll sort him out once and for all.'

Stella had confided to me that her mother was very ill with a condition called multiple sclerosis. The M.S. was gradually making her more and more disabled. As her condition had deteriorated, her husband, Stella's father, had left them, unable to cope with the prospect of nursing a dying woman. He had moved to the other side of the island with another woman, had another child and Stella hadn't seen him since.

Virtually housebound, Stella's mother used crutches to get around the flat and there was a small shabby wheelchair folded up by the door. It fell to Stella to care for her mother, do the shopping, cooking and cleaning as well as attending school and earning money. That was why she'd ended up having the misfortune of working for Stephan, her father's brother.

'Don't worry mama, I'm a hard worker. I will find another job, especially with the tourist season in full swing and we will be fine. If Stephan even tries to make trouble or bad mouth me to the other taverna and bar owners, I will threaten to report him to the police. I'll also post all the sordid details of his abuse on social media, so I'm sure he'll keep quiet. When I finish at school and have my qualifications, I'll be able to get a really respectable job. So, you see you mustn't worry… But mama,' she hesitated.

'There's something else I have to tell you… I have the dog here that saved me, he's here in the apartment.'

'Oh Stella, a dog? We can't keep him here.' Her mother said anxiously. 'You know the rules; no pets allowed. We could be evicted if anyone finds out.'

'Mama his name is Alexis and he's faithful and brave and he's my hero.' Stella said sweetly but firmly.

'Alexis! Come here boy!' She called softly. I crept in slowly, wagging my tail and put my paw up on the bed next to her mother. She was a fragile older lady with grey hair tied up in a bun and an unhealthy pale pallor.

I gave her my best 'loving dog' expression, hoping to touch her heart.

Her mother recoiled in alarm. 'Stella, what are you thinking? That is a hunting hound, bred to work, not a pet or house dog and he's black. You know black dogs bring bad luck. No, you must find him another place to go as soon as possible. He cannot stay here! I know he did a brave thing standing up to Stephan, but our landlord will make no exceptions. The dog has to go, and go he must, as soon as possible!'

'But mama, he's such a kind, gentle soul, how can I abandon him after what he did to save me?' She implored. 'He isn't just a hound, he has a soul and a wonderful nature. I don't believe that black dogs are bad luck either, that's just old fashioned, ignorant superstition which does no one any favours! I won't see him ending up in the dreadful municipal dog pound with all the other strays, being half starved and beaten every day. I can't do that to him mama! I won't! I won't!'

Stella's mother capitulated and reluctantly agreed that I could stay in the apartment for just one night, but we slept fitfully. We all knew that Stephan could turn up with the police at any time because of what I'd done.

However, I was grateful to have the opportunity to sleep under a solid roof with walls and comfort for once and best of all, to be near to my sweet Stella. I knew I'd do absolutely anything for her and my heart was, for that moment at least, content.

Chapter 9

True to her word, Stella was up early, stealthily taking me downstairs, before anyone could notice and went in search of another job. She'd tied her hair up into a ponytail and dressed in a pretty yellow polka dot dress. I trotted proudly beside her from one bar to another and taverna to taverna, waiting patiently outside until she came out.

By lunchtime, she'd secured employment at an upmarket fish restaurant near the centre of town starting the next evening and could hardly contain her excitement or wait to tell her mother the thrilling news.

As we neared the apartment block it became clear that I wouldn't be able to gain entry: There were too many people about and we couldn't risk being reported to the tenant's association or landlord. Stella turned back, hiding her face and cutting up the street at the side of the building and down an alley way to a door, leading into the underground space below the shops and flats.
'I can hide you in the basement for now and maybe for a while.' She whispered while she tried the door. 'Only the refuse collectors go in there and I'm sure we'd find a quiet, cozy corner for you to hide in.'

The door was locked.

'Wait here Alexis, I'll fetch the key from the apartment. Back soon!' She said. And off my girl sped.

I waited and watched. A white van drew up at the end of the alley and two scruffy men got out. One was tall and lanky, with a greasy mop of black hair and the other was a short, squat man with beefy arms who had an exaggerated, arrogant stance that warned the world to back off.
Instead of unloading produce and merchandise for the shops as I expected, the lanky man brought out a large metal pole with a loop at one end and, with the short man guarding that end of the alley, he marched up towards me. Instinct told me that this was not going to be a friendly encounter, so I turned and ran away from the perceived danger.

Springing over boxes and refuse sacks, I sprinted in the opposite direction and came to an abrupt halt: There was a high brick wall with no way over or through! A dead end! There was no escape!

The loop quickly fastened around my neck and closed in on my throat like a vice! I tried to wriggle and squirm my way out of the metal grasper but struggling just caused the loop to get tighter. It was useless; I was trapped and choking for breath.

The tall, lanky man dragged me roughly down the alley towards the van. Resistance was useless, even though I tried to stop myself by digging my claws down into the crevices between the paving slabs of the path. As we neared the van, the squat, muscular man opened the door a few inches. 'We've got ourselves a feisty one here Stavros!'

Before I knew it, I was thrust through the small opening, the grasper released and the door slammed shut.

On the opposite street corner, I'd noticed, just for a split second, a third man standing by; he had a bandaged arm and an evil sneer on his face. It was Stephan!

I looked around, desperately seeking an escape, only to find three sets of frightened eyes looking at me through the dim light. There were other dogs here too. Two were hunting dogs; pointers, both so thin you could see every rib through their scabby coats.

The other was a medium sized dog, whose eyes seemed familiar to me even though they oozed with yellow pus. His skin, almost devoid of fur, was covered in a thickening mass of sores and welts.

It was mange, caused by burrowing parasites that live in the skin and feed on the blood of the victim. These microscopic mites had compelled the pitiful dog to scratch itself raw with the deep irritation. It was a horrible condition to be in. He cowered in the corner of the van and had urinated in fear, adding to the already foul stench inside the van.

Realising there was something I recognised about the mangy dog, I slowly crept towards him and whined. The poor dog distracted for a moment from his scratching, looked up and wagged his tail weakly. It was him! As I saw through his disfigured face and body, I recognised my dear brother Apollo! What joy!

He was equally as elated to see me and we licked each other gently, renewing our bond and my heart leapt with happiness to be reunited with my big brother. His condition worried me though and I couldn't imagine the pain he was suffering. We needed to get help for him as soon as possible. But from where?

The overcrowded van journeyed on stopping once again. Two more dogs were forced through the door to join us in the back. These dogs were also terrified and in a terrible condition; a small black female poodle cross who looked as if she was expecting pups and a large tan male Jura hound with a deep, bleeding wound to his side. What a sorry lot we were: Unloved, forlorn and forgotten.

My heart was bereft.

Chapter 10

A while later the van came to a stop and we heard the clanking of chains and the scraping of a large gate being opened. The van moved forward a few metres and stopped. The gate closed and the two men got out and walked away, slamming the doors behind them.

'Time for a bite to eat I reckon.' One said.

I tried to peer through the small window at the back, but it was too dirty to see through. There were the disconcerting sounds of several dogs barking, howling and whining outside and the little poodle cross, distressed and by now trembling, urinated and defecated in the van.

Where was everyone? It was now late spring and the temperature of the midday sun was rising and still no one came to let us out or water our parched mouths. Panting hard, in an effort to cool our overheating bodies, the atmosphere was stagnant with putrid air and oppressive heat. The injured Jura hound collapsed at one corner of the van, listless and almost unconscious. The other dogs whined and whimpered and Apollo was scratching relentlessly at his already bloodied, raw skin.

We needed to get out of this van and quickly!

I heard voices in the distance amid the constant barking from other dogs outside, so started to scratch and bark at the back door of the van, hoping to attract someone's attention. We could hardly breathe and needed help. After what seemed forever, the back doors were finally flung open.

All suffering from heat exhaustion and dehydration; the sensation of relatively fresh air rushing into the van was extremely welcome.

'Right dogs! Let's be having you! Out you come! Phew...what a stink!'

It was Stavros.

Hesitantly, we all jumped down from the van. All except the injured Jura Hound whom Stavros dragged out and left in a heap on the ground. Horror struck I realised that we were now in the middle of the notorious and much dreaded, municipal dog pound.

This wasn't just bad, it was disastrous!

The noise from the resident dogs, excited at the prospect of a few new arrivals, was almost deafening and feeling disorientated, we just stood there, trembling, trying to take in our new surroundings:

Around the yard were probably ten small cages. Each one contained several dogs of varying breeds, colours and sizes but most were hunting breeds, Jura Hounds, pointers and Greek hare hounds like myself, all standing amidst their own mess.

The smell was awful. Each cage had a wooden shelf to offer a little shade from the heat but as the sun moved around, even that was inadequate and there was no comfort in evidence at all.

We, new arrivals, had a rope slung around our necks and Stavros dragged each dog to a cage and pushed us in to join the awaiting incumbents.

The incessant barking was almost frenzied now and as I entered the cage with Apollo, the other dogs rushed forward to check us out. It was the same for the other new arrivals and the pregnant poodle cross bitch was shoved into the cage next to me, containing several dogs who were twice her size.

Suddenly a savage fight broke out between two dogs with another one piling in to attack an emaciated pointer bitch, who squealed and screamed in pain as they tore into her.

'Hey! Stop that!' Stavros yelled, as he directed a strong jet of water from a hose onto the fighting dogs who retreated, leaving the pointer bitch to lick her wounds.

I stood quietly while the other dogs in our cage sniffed us over and then went back to lying in any available shade. Gratefully, I noticed a bucket of water from which I and Apollo drank our fill, despite the layer of green, putrid slime at the bottom. Water was water after all and we were desperately thirsty.

Life in the dog pound was life on the edge. At any moment fights between dogs could break out: Living in such close confinement with each other meant constant competition for food. Bitches in season and unneutered males, placed in the same cage was a recipe for disaster and aggression frequently spilled out, due to the lack of physical and mental stimulation. It was hard to relax. Flash points regularly occurred during feeding times and when new dogs arrived.

Food was sparse and a rare commodity; a meal every three days was all we were given if we were lucky. The pups, ill, injured and smaller dogs rarely stood a chance of getting a share and they went without, becoming thinner and weaker by the day.

Diseases and parasites were constant companions and dogs died from otherwise preventable and curable illnesses but, as pound dogs, we soon realized that we were worth less than nothing and veterinary care was a luxury we were not worthy of.

My cage was inhabited by four other dogs as well as Apollo and myself. Luckily, we were all of a similar size and good natured: Being pack animals, hunting dogs usually get along with other dogs well and one of our companions was a young, sweet, mixed breed bitch. She was black and tan like me but had the most stunningly vivid blue eyes that seemed to pierce and paralyze my heart. She was so beautiful. She was certainly a most welcome distraction during my time in the pound.

However, my main concern was for my brother Apollo: What little bit of food I managed to get hold of, I shared with him. I could see his condition was insufferable and worsening by the day and there was nothing I could do about it. I felt wretched.

One day, as Stavros was leaving the pound, a younger man with curly brown hair and twinkling eyes arrived at the pound. I saw him giving some money to Stavros in exchange for some keys.

'You here again Andreas?' Stavros asked. 'I don't understand your affection for these disease-ridden mutts. They're just dogs. Still, if you want to waste your time and money on them, that's up to you I suppose. Madness, I call it! Right, I'm off home. Lock up when you go!'

Andreas looked around the cages and set to work cleaning them out and bringing in some extra sacks of dog food. He had a gentle kindness about him and talked to the dogs as he went about his tasks.

Some days, Stavros didn't come to the pound at all. Unless Andreas came, we were without food, standing in our own mess and drinking foul stagnant water, tainted with urine and excrement.

In the adjoining cage to ours, was the pretty little poodle cross who had arrived with me and I could sense that her pups were due imminently. She was panting and pacing around the cage, licking her lips and would alternately lie in any available shade and then pace around again. That night, she took herself into a corner of the cage and went into labour.

By early morning, four tiny pups had been born onto the hard, comfortless floor and were suckling milk from their mother.

She had also found a friend in a big, amiable black and white pointer who stood watching over her all night, as she toiled through the birth.
He gently nuzzled her fur as she fed her babies and she licked his nose in gratitude.

We watched this almost biblical scene and were relieved that the little dog had come through the labour without any complications. The other co-habitants of her cage stayed apart from them, as if respecting this miracle of nature and my heart was glad.

Chapter 11

Every day, more dogs would arrive at the pound and soon the cages were full to bursting. The young lad, Andreas, would bring a bit of extra food around, fill the bucket with the hosepipe and jet wash the cages, sending diluted urine and excrement up into the air which splattered over our bodies and sullied our fur. He couldn't help it; the pound was so overcrowded that there was nowhere else to put us while he swilled the floor.

Sadly, within a couple of days, the little pups in the next cage fell ill and although Andreas tried to help them, one by one they died. Their mother, the little poodle cross died soon after and Andreas tenderly removed their lifeless bodies, burying them on a patch of waste ground next to the pound, tears in his eyes. All we could do was watch on, grief in our hearts.

A few days after we arrived, a blue car arrived on the site and a brusque, business like woman got out carrying a large black case and went into the cabin. Several dogs; three pointers, two hare hounds and a small terrier who'd been in the pound for a couple of weeks, were dragged from their cages, ropes around their necks by Stavros.

Some of them resisted and were kicked or beaten harshly, yelping and crying out in pain. Most were too weary, weak with hunger or illness to resist. They all went through the cabin door, never to return. Their places in the cages were soon filled by other dogs brought in from the streets. It was never ending.

A pickup truck came the next day and we witnessed black sacks being flung on to the back and driven away. I never saw a single dog come back out of the cabin alive, and the air smelt of decay, despondency and death.

The mood in the pound was sombre. It was as if all the dogs sensed that they were living on borrowed time. The only little ray of light was the lad with the twinkling eyes who cared for us but Stavros just belittled him for his kindness.

'They're just dogs after all!' He would remark scathingly.

Early one morning, Andreas came in, carefully carrying a cardboard box.
'Hey, Stavros! Someone has left this box of little puppies by the gate. They can't be more than three or four weeks old. What should I do with them? The cages are all too full and these pups wouldn't survive in there anyway.'

Stavros was standing idly at the door to the cabin, smoking a cigarette. 'Just leave them in here, there's nothing you can do, with any luck they'll die soon anyway.'

The twinkling eyes of the lad suddenly looked crestfallen but he did as he'd been told.

Later, after Stavros had gone and Andreas was giving us some much-appreciated food, he stopped and took out his mobile phone.

'Hi there! Can I speak to Anna please? Oh, yes, hello Anna, my name's Andreas and I'm calling from the local municipal dog pound. I'm a volunteer here, just trying to make life a bit more bearable for the dogs, you know, cleaning the cages and giving them a bit of extra food when I can afford it. The pound owner makes me pay him for coming in, but most days he leaves me the keys and I can stay as long as I want to. The thing is Anna, we've got some young pups that need help. I know you and your friends try to help these dogs too and I wondered if there's anything you can do? Yes, that's right.'

He listened attentively. 'Ok, great. Yes, I'll wait here for you. Thank you so much. See you later.'

He put his phone back into his pocket and continued feeding the other dogs, whistling a little tune. He looked happy. We were all fond of Andreas.

That afternoon, a large white estate car drew up outside and a man and woman in their early thirties got out and came to the gate. They both looked concerned and the woman's pretty dark eyes were dewy with tears. Andreas let them in, chatting to them amiably and handed over the cardboard box containing the pups, which they inspected and placed carefully into the car. Then they returned and turned their attention to the cages where we were all housed.

Andreas was talking. 'Yes, of course Anna that would fantastic. Any dogs you can take the better. It's full to bursting as you can see. There are some that are due to be euthanized on Monday too. Stavros had five put to sleep last week as well.' He said sadly, tears in his eyes.

Anna looked angry and shook her head of mahogany curls.

'Oh Marios!' she seethed to her male companion 'It's sickening. I just can't understand how people can abandon and treat these wonderful creatures with such cruel disdain!'

Marios put his arms around her and held her to him.

'Well, let's see what we can do to help, let's start by looking around and take the one's we can.' He said soothingly, wiping away her tears.

They all walked around the pound together, slowly. The lad, man and woman in sole purpose, talking to the dogs and offering treats of food through the bars. Some dogs cowered in fear and others approached them, cautiously optimistic and grateful for the extra sustenance. Many just craved human contact and relished the touch of a hand and kind word.

'Marios we can only afford to take four dogs out today, we've nowhere to put more than that. We owe money at the private kennels and all our lovely foster homes are already over stretched. We've the puppies to consider too, so that's eight. It's just heart breaking.' Anna sighed.

'I know Anna but we do what we can. Four saved is better than none. We need to be strong.' Marios asserted.

'Andreas, do you know which dogs are on the put to sleep list for Monday?' Anna asked.

Andreas gestured towards me and Apollo, the two pointers and injured Jura hound who had come at the same time.
I wagged my tail and poked my nose through the bars of the cage. I wanted so much to live and could sense these were good people. I felt instinctively that I could trust them, despite everything I had been through.

'This dog is such a sweetheart.' Anna said, putting her hand through the cage to stroke my head. We can get him into foster quite quickly. The mange infested dog is another matter and will take a lot of time and resources to get well again and funds are so low Marios. I feel awful leaving him here but we're so short of money, we just can't take him…. Andreas, we'll take the two pointers, this Greek hare hound and the injured Jura hound, he just needs cleaning up and some antibiotics…. that's our four. I feel awful leaving the others though. It's just terrible!' She said, bursting into tears once again.

'Ok,' she said, regaining her composure and drying her eyes. 'Can you help us get them on leads and into the car please Andreas?'

Andreas came into the cage and slipped a rope leash over my head and started to lead me out of the cage, towards the gate. I dug my paws into the hard ground and refused to move.

'Come on boy, you're being saved. These kind people will look after you, come on.' He said, encouragingly.

But still I refused to budge.

'What's the problem Andreas' Marios called from across the yard.
'It's this Greek hare hound, he won't come out of the cage!' Andreas replied.

Anna and Marios came over, holding the other three dogs on leads. 'Ok,' Anna said curiously, 'just drop the lead and let's see what he does.'

Instantly, I went to the back of the cage and stood by my brother Apollo.
'That's interesting,' Andreas mused, 'those two dogs have been inseparable while they've been here. Sharing food and sleeping side by side. It's as if one depends on the other.'

'Right, well then…' Anna conceded, 'we'll have to take them both, that's all there is to it. We'll just have to figure out what we're going to do with him that's all, and I'll beg, borrow or even steal the money to treat his skin.'

And, so it was, that this wonderful, kind hearted couple removed me and my brother Apollo from the hell hole of the dog pound in the nick of time and my heart dared to be hopeful.

Chapter 12

The first port of call was a trip to the vet. He was a jolly, chubby man with a shock of grey white hair and a luxuriant curly beard, decorating his red cheeked face.

'Hello, you two life savers!' He said jovially, as he greeted Anna and Marios with their cache of sorry looking dogs and the cardboard box with its precious pups.
'Another few souls rescued today then?' He chuckled.
With that, he tenderly examined the puppies followed by me, Apollo and the three other adult dogs.

'Well,' he said, washing his hands under the tap. 'They all have fleas and ticks as you're probably aware, so we'll need to treat those. They're all severely undernourished and we'll have to get the adult dogs vaccinated against all the usual diseases. The dog with mange will need bathing two to three times a week with a special anti-parasitic shampoo and antibiotics for the infection. It will take a lot of dedication but he should be fine in a couple of months.

The Jura hound's wound needs cleaning up and a couple of stitches. The pups are too young to vaccinate and to be frank, you'll have your work cut out getting them through the next few weeks. Don't you have a nursing bitch feeding her own pups in foster care at the moment?' Anna nodded in agreement 'I thought so. Perhaps that bitch might, with the right encouragement, adopt these little pups as well which would give them a better chance. God knows what's become of their mother but it's highly likely that she died of untreated pyometra, a serious infection of the womb, hence the dumping of the pups.'

'How much is all this this going to cost Markus?' asked Marios anxiously. 'The charity is so short of funds at the moment.'

'Don't you worry about that young fella,' the vet chortled. 'Let us just agree that you'll give me what you can, when you can, and say no more. I know how much you and your friends do to help these poor dogs and I take my hat off to you! I know you'll pay me when you can.'
'Oh, thank you so much Markus' whispered Anna gratefully, almost sobbing with the relief. 'You are so good, thank you.' She hugged the affable vet and gave him a peck on the cheek.

A little embarrassed by this overt show of affection he gave a little cough, and replied:

'It's you two who are good Anna, without your efforts and organization these poor dogs wouldn't stand a chance. I recognise that we can't save them all and change the world, but if you can change the world for each dog you save, then that in itself, is a truly wonderful thing.'

As we were each treated for the parasites and injected against disease we stood patiently, accepting that this was helping us and we all trusted this kindly vet with his big gentle hands and deep soothing voice.
Leaving an hour or so later we were put back into the car and set off, Marios driving and Anna on the phone.

'Hi Pete, it's Anna here. You and Kate ok? That's good… Listen we've just picked up five dogs and four pups from the pound, taken them to the vet and are desperate to find foster places for them. I know it's asking a lot, what with all the animals you have already but, is there any chance you can help out?.... You can?.... How many can you take?.... Two? Brilliant!.... That's fantastic, thank you so much Pete. We'll be with you in about forty minutes. See you soon. Bye for now.'

Another couple of calls secured foster places for us all and a foster mother for the pups. 'That's great Anna!' Marios said, a huge grin across his handsome face. 'Well done! What a relief!'

But Anna was defiant 'Yes, it's great for these dogs, Marios, but for every dog we rescue, hundreds more suffer and die and it breaks my heart. Why do the hunters treat these poor souls with such callous disregard? My God, they take more time and trouble looking after their trucks and rifles than their dogs. I just don't get it. They shoot them, break their legs, hang them from trees or just abandon them when they've finished with them, like pieces of garbage. They think hounds don't have feelings and don't see the beauty and nobility of these dogs. They use them, abuse them and get rid of them. It makes me so angry.'

Anna was really infuriated. 'Some people in this country have no moral compass and our work will never end, unless we can change people's attitudes to these hounds. It's the children we need to reach out to, get into schools, give presentations, take in some of our rescue dogs and show them how wonderful they are and that what's going on is simply wrong on so many levels!'

'You're right Anna, we can look into doing just that. I know one of the teachers at our local school. I'm sure she'll help us put an educational programme together. We'll start there and then, hopefully, that will get the ball rolling around the island. It will take time but as the saying goes, Rome wasn't built in a day and we have to start somewhere.' Marios suggested.

Shortly, we arrived at a large villa on the outskirts of another town. Aeroplanes were flying overhead and once we got through the large secure gate, we were greeted by a woman with a cloud of curly blonde hair surrounding her face and a tall middle-aged man with a neat beard and blue eyes accompanied by a large pack of dogs who were milling around them, eager to greet us new arrivals.

'Hi Kate, Hi Pete!' called Anna 'Thanks for helping out again, we're so grateful.'
'No problem at all Anna.' Pete replied. 'You know us, crazy English! We've stayed out too long in the midday sun I reckon!'

They all laughed.

And so, Apollo and I found ourselves with this animal loving, slightly mad but passionate couple Kate and Pete. They had moved to Cyprus from the UK to work and had opened their hearts and home to countless abandoned and damaged dogs and cats over the years. Their house and land was ours to call our own.

Truly, I couldn't believe my luck and I tried to show my gratitude every day by being as good as a hound could be. Apollo and I soon settled in to our new life of luxury, very willingly! We slept on the sofas whenever we pleased, chewed their shoes and cushions and at night jostled for the best spot on Kate and Pete's enormous bed; dogs, cats and humans together, sleeping in perfect harmony and mutual adoration.

This blissful existence was reminiscent of my puppyhood and I felt secure and safe again. There was no need to worry about food and clear fresh water was in constant supply.

It really was dog heaven and my heart rejoiced!

Chapter 13

Kate was s a great fan of old black and white movies as well as Hollywood musicals and every evening, after tending to our needs, we would all pile onto the big sofas with Pete and Kate to watch a DVD of an old film. All the animals at the villa received names reflecting this passion of hers and I was duly christened Crosby, after the famous actor and singer Bing Crosby. My brother became Charlie, named after the comedy actor Charlie Chaplin. Other names bestowed upon members of our new large fur family included Brynner, Cagney, Betty, Olivia, Rita, Roddy, Brando, and Flynn. To be honest, we were treated like Hollywood royalty too and life couldn't have been better.

In this dreamland, it was hard to imagine anything was wrong with the world but after a couple of weeks, I awoke feeling a little under the weather: I started being sick, had bouts of diarrhea and felt very weary and lethargic. I was off my food, which for me, was unheard of and all my limbs ached dreadfully.

Kate and Pete were quick to act and Pete drove me the forty-minute journey back to Markus the jolly, bearded vet we'd seen before. He examined me carefully with his expert hands, looking into my eyes, ears and mouth and took my temperature.

'I suspect this lad has ehrlichiosis Pete. Without a blood test, I can't be sure of course, but if it is, without treatment, the prognosis is pretty poor I'm afraid and could prove fatal.'

'What's ehrlichiosis?' Pete enquired, alarmed.

'It's a nasty tick born bacterial organism passed, to the dog when the tick bites it. It attacks the white blood cells and causes all these symptoms and other potential neurological problems which can lead to lameness and lack of coordination. Ultimately, it can cause organ failure and death.'

'Good grief Markus, that sounds awful. Ok, let's do the blood test and investigate the cause, we can't leave him like this.' Pete urged.

I just stood there feeling depressed, head down and nauseous. I really didn't care when Markus stuck the needle into my leg to take some blood. He was welcome to it.

'I'm going to keep him in overnight Pete. He's very dehydrated, so may need to go on a saline drip and I'll give him something to alleviate the feeling of sickness. The blood test results should be back tomorrow and if it is what I suspect, we'll get him started on some antibiotics immediately, which he will need to take for a few weeks.'
I was given the injection and had a drip put into my leg linked to a pouch of saline solution. I hardly slept that night but by morning I was starting to feel marginally better although still weary and achy.

'How're you doing fella?' asked the vet the next day, patting my head softly 'Any better? Pete will be coming to take you home soon.'

When Pete arrived, I listened as the vet confirmed that I was suffering with ehrlichiosis and prescribed the course of antibiotics and regular check-ups to make sure that I was responding to treatment.

Back at the villa, Pete explained it all to Kate. 'It's a damn good thing that Anna and Marios took him out of the dog pound, isn't it? Even if he'd avoided euthanasia there, he wouldn't have lived much longer with this disease.'

'You're right Pete. Thank goodness he's safe now. He's such a sweet natured dog, it would have been a crime to let him suffer and die.' Kate reflected sadly.

Gradually, over the next few weeks, I improved and was soon back to my old self. The only external signs of ever having had the ehrlichiosis was a slightly lolloping walk, due to the neurological damage caused by the disease but I wasn't in any pain and still enjoyed running around like a mad thing, playing with the other dogs in the large enclosure behind the villa.

The animal angels that Kate and Pete were meant they invariably saved and fostered other dogs and cats during our time with them. Some dogs and cats left the villa to go to somewhere they called a 'forever home' which Kate and Pete always looked pleased about.

One such new arrival, was a young emaciated pup who Kate had found abandoned on the roadside, infested with fleas and ticks. Kate named her Ava, after the celebrated and beautiful 1940's actress Ava Gardner. The pup's name was well chosen, as she grew into a real beauty too.

She was black and tan like me but with the most stunning azure blue eyes and my heart was totally smitten.

Chapter 14

Time passed contentedly and the hardships endured in the past were eased by the generous warmth and love showered upon us every day by Kate and Pete. One day Kate's phone rang and it was Anna who had rescued me from the pound.

'Hi Anna, how are you? Really? Congratulations, that lovely news. Just a second.... Hey Pete? It's Anna on the phone, she's got engaged to Marios! Isn't that fab! ...Hi Anna. Yes, yes that's right. Crosby is fully recovered now. I think it's about time we started to think about rehoming him and Charlie, don't you?... Yes, of course I will, no problem. You take care. See you soon. Bye for now.'

Looking down at me, Kate smiled, angling her camera phone in front of her. 'Time for your close-up Bing Crosby, say sausages!'

She pressed something on her phone and examined it. 'Yup! That's a great photo. If that doesn't get you snapped up in a new forever home soon, I'm a monkey! We'll put your picture and a little description onto the rescue's website and I'll put you on my social media page too. You never know Crosby? Your new home could be just a heartbeat away! Your turn Charlie Chaplin!' She turned to my brother and pressed her phone, checked it and smiled.

'Another excellent photo!' She said, patting our heads before going off into the kitchen, to get our food ready.

Days passed in tranquil contentment. Playing, eating, relaxing then playing again. It was a hard life!

Then, the landline phone rang and Kate answered:

'Yes, this is Kate. Oh, hello Jenny thanks for ringing. What can I tell you? His name's Crosby, but you know that from the website.'

My ears pricked up instantly at the mention of my name. 'He's about one year old, possible eighteen months. He was a pound dog rescued in the nick of time and brought into foster with us by some wonderful people who help these abused dogs.

He has a wonderful sweet nature, loves everyone, especially children, so we suspect he grew up within a family. He's house trained, hardly ever barks and sleeps through the night with no problem, gets on great with other animals and is just a super all round dog. We're not sure how he is off lead, as all the dogs here have the run of the place, but he's young enough to learn… Sure, I'll wait to hear back from you…. Thanks for ringing. Bye for now.'

She ruffled the fur on my neck. 'Well Crosby, that was a nice lady called Jenny ringing all the way from England and she and her husband are interested in adopting you! They have a little girl and two other dogs so you'd still have some playmates too. How exciting!'

I wagged my tail. 'Woof!'

'Hey there! I just told her that you hardly ever bark, don't go letting me down now!' She laughed.

Later that day Kate and Pete were talking about the arrangements for my rehoming while we were all snuggled up together.

'You know how close Crosby and Charlie are Pete? There's something about their relationship that makes me wonder if they're related in some way. Wouldn't it be brilliant if we could rehome them together? Do you know what? I'm going to call that lady who's interested in Crosby and ask her to consider doing just that.'

The next day Kate rang Jenny and talked it over with her:

'Crosby has a really close bond with another dog here called Charlie. They were in the municipal pound together and apparently, Crosby wouldn't leave Charlie behind to go with Anna and Marios. So, as you can imagine we'd love to see them rehomed together if at all possible… Can you think it over, discuss it with your family and get back to me?... Lovely. That's super. We'll speak soon. Bye for now.'

Within a couple of hours, the phone rang again and Kate answered:

'Hello? Oh, Hi Jenny…. really? That's a really fantastic solution... Wait until I tell Pete the brilliant news! Thank you so much Jenny. We'll be in touch as soon as possible and arrange the home checks and transport for both dogs… Bye for now.'

'Pete, Pete!' she called. 'Guess what? That was Jenny from the UK. Sadly, her sister-in-law's dog has recently passed away aged fifteen and they're looking for another dog and have agreed to adopt Charlie! Crosby and Charlie would live half an hour away from each other and see each other every weekend, it's a perfect scenario! I'm so happy I could cry!'

Within a few days, Charlie and I had had another trip to the vet to get our special pet passports. I was to fly to the UK three weeks later, followed by Charlie the following week.

The big day arrived and I was placed in a large plastic travel crate with blankets and water and driven to the airport. I was sad to leave my brother behind but somehow, I knew we'd meet again.

Kate and Pete were a little tearful when they said their goodbyes to me too but I could tell they were happy tears.

'Be a good boy Crosby, you're going to your lovely forever home today and you'll see Charlie again very soon too! It's the beginning of the rest of your wonderful new life boy. Be happy big man. Goodbye.'

They both kissed my wet nose through the bars of the crate door and the conveyer belt going up into the hold of the aeroplane slowly carried me away from Pete and Kate.

It was a bittersweet parting as I was so grateful to them for all they'd done for me but my heart was full of anticipation.

Chapter 15

Somewhere in England, UK.

The journey on the plane from Cyprus to England took a long time. I wasn't the only dog on board and some of the others barked and whined amid the unfamiliar environment and strange smells. For me? Well, I was characteristically chilled about it and settled down, nestling into the warm blankets and was soon fast asleep. By the time the plane landed, I was feeling hungry and desperate for a wee! The crate trundled out of the plane on the conveyer belt and was loaded onto a trailer and taken to a large building on the periphery of the airport.

 I sniffed the air. It was evening and the air was a lot cooler and fresher than the air I'd left behind in Cyprus. Between the noise of planes and the other dogs whining and barking, I could hear voices through the door to the building and eventually a cheerful lady with close cropped blond hair, wearing a blue uniform, came along and opened the crate door a little.

'Hi there doggy, are you Crosby?' She patted my head and scanned my microchip, checked over some paperwork and called out. 'Ok Jack, this one is clear to go!'

I felt someone else dragging my crate along the floor, through a door and out into the open on the other side. There was a dozen or more people waiting around.

'Dog for Willis! Dog for Willis!' A man's voice announced.

Almost immediately, I found I was looking through the crate door at a woman with long dark hair, blue eyes and a big smile. 'Hello Crosby, welcome to England.' She said gently. 'Let's get you out of there, you must be bursting for a pee!'
She opened the crate, clipped a leash onto my collar and caressed my head. Although I felt a little disorientated and uncertain, I followed her over to a small area of grass, where I peed for England, Cyprus and the rest of world. What a relief!

'Mummy, mummy let me hold him. Please!' It was a pretty young girl of about ten or eleven, with the same dark hair and smile as her mother.

'Ok Molly, he's quite strong, so hold the lead tightly.' The girl bent down and looked me in the eye and kissed my nose. 'Hello gorgeous boy. We're going to be the bestest friends ever. I just know it!'

The attraction between us was spontaneous and as I looked into her sweet eyes I knew that at last, I had come home. I licked her dear face as she hugged me and I could feel her little heart beating beneath mine.

The woman with the smiley face and her husband, a tall bespectacled, bearded man. who patted my head and tickled behind my ears, struggled to take the crate apart and fit it into the back of their not insubstantially sized car. Molly just carried on hugging and kissing me as if there was no tomorrow.

Wow! I decided. I liked England!

'Good grief, this crate is enormous!' The man exclaimed. 'There's no room for the dog Jenny!' He joked.

It was about a half hour car journey to my new home in England. Molly sat with me and talked to me all the way and stroked my fur reassuringly. I put my paw into her little hand and some deep memory stirred of another child who had loved me too and suddenly everything fell into place: All that I had been through had brought me to this little girl and I knew that I was never going to let her go.

We arrived at their modest but comfortable home in the late evening, where I was introduced to their two other dogs; Otto, a cheeky Yorkshire terrier and Toby a mongrel of indeterminable parentage, who appraised me with a critical eye then proceeded to steadfastly ignore me.

'What name shall we give our dapper new dog Molly? It seems to me that he's got a new home, a new life, so needs a new name to complete the hat trick…so what do you think?' Bill asked.

'I'm not sure,' puzzled Molly, 'he's so lovely and handsome he needs a name that suits him perfectly. We'll have to think about it. How about if tomorrow, we each write our ideas for a new name on a piece of paper, fold them, put them in a bag and pick one out?'

'Good idea Molly, let's do just that… Right, it's time for bed everyone. It's already late and I've got work tomorrow and you've got school Molly!'

'Can Crosby sleep in my room tonight Dad? Please?' Molly implored.
'Alright. But only tonight. After that, he stays downstairs with Otto and Toby at bedtime. Ok?'

'Ok.' Said Molly giving me a 'we'll-see-about-that' little wink.

'Bed, Crosby!'

I followed my girl up the stairs and my heart was truly enraptured.

Chapter 16

Early next morning we were all allowed out into the lovely big garden for a toilet break and then back into the house for our first meal of the day. The family sat at the table eating breakfast and then they each put their pieces of paper, with their name suggestions into a carrier bag. Molly closed her eyes and picked one out. She unfolded the paper carefully and her eyes lit up.

'Hector! That was my suggestion! Whoopee! Hector my gorgeous hare hound!' She flung her arms around my neck and hugged me.

'You are hereby named Hector Willis.' She announced solemnly.'
'May you be loved, happy and healthy for the rest of your life!'

Jenny and Bill exchanged a wry smile and cheered.

'Hear, Hear! Here's to Hector!' They clunked their mugs of tea, smiling.

'Live long and happy!'

I wagged my tail in agreement. 'Woof!'

Soon it was time to go out on our first official walk together. I'd noticed as soon as I'd seen the garden that it had a high fence and secure gate at the bottom of the path, beyond which I could see a large number of trees. Eager to explore, my curiosity was at last satisfied when Molly and Jenny took us out through the gate. Otto and Toby, the lucky pair, were allowed off the lead, running around free, for there, right on our doorstep, was a wonderful playground of woods, water and footpaths frequented by people, dogs, ducks, pigeons, rabbits and squirrels.

My olfactory system was in happiness overload with all the wonderful smells around me. I was desperate to be released; I longed to run and chase through the woods and undergrowth with Otto and Toby. It was part of my DNA to hunt and I itched to be off the lead and following wherever my nose took me!

'He's so eager to go Bill,' Jenny remarked over dinner that evening, 'but we can't risk letting him off lead just yet. We'll have to do some doggy recall training with him first.'

The very next week we attended our first dog training class alongside dogs and owners of all shapes and sizes. What great fun we had, and to top it all, whenever I got something right I got a tasty piece of chicken. What's not to love?

Soon I could sit, stay, wait, lie down, and stand to command and once more, distant memories of a little boy who'd loved me and trained me sprang to mind and caressed my heart.

Coming back when called was another matter though! I just wanted to be off, sniffing all the amazing scents around about me. Out on our twice daily walks I was still on lead and yearned to be off. After about two months of recall training on a long lead, the time came to try me off the lead at last.

'Ok, this is the moment of truth Hector.' Jenny said, as she unclipped the lead from my collar. 'Be a good boy!'

At last! I had a taste of freedom. I ran and romped. I chased and charged. Up and down, through the woods, through the brook and along the paths. It was a Greek hare hound's paradise.

What joy! Racing through those woods and paths. I got so carried away that I became totally absorbed in my exploration and became deaf to the calls and whistles from Jenny and Molly as I continued to rummage and root around, taking in the mirage of scents and smells.

I ran and ran and tracked and trailed every scent I could find.

Suddenly I realised there was something missing. My family!

Looking around, I realised there was nobody there, although I could still hear them calling me, away in the distance.

Home! I must go home! My paws hardly touched the ground as I flew back! The house backed onto a conservation area, so there were no busy roads anywhere and I was quickly and safely by the back gate to the garden.
It was closed. No problem I thought, I'll just sit here and wait.

Just then, a local man we knew well came along walking his own dogs and noticed me sitting by the gate. 'Locked out Hector?' He said smiling, as he opened it for me. I wagged my tail. 'There you go boy.'

I ran in happily and he closed the gate behind me. Where was everybody? I barked and scratched at the back door. Nothing… yet I could still hear them calling me. Perturbed, I ran back to the gate and barked as loudly as I could. 'Woof! Woof!' I'm here! I'm here!

Eventually, I heard my family getting closer and closer and soon after, Jenny and Molly arrived with Otto and Toby. I flung myself at Molly as soon as she came through the gate, almost knocking her to the ground. I was overjoyed to be reunited with her; bouncing up and down and wagging my tail. 'Woof!'

'Oh Hector, we thought we'd lost you boy!' Molly cried, hugging me to her as if she'd never let me go. Please don't run off again boy, we love you too much to lose you now. Thank goodness you know your way home and Bob saw you waiting by the gate!'

I couldn't explain that I hadn't run off to get away from them, I'd just become engrossed in the thrill of the chase, but from that day on I never let my family and especially Molly out of my sight:

Wherever I was and no matter what I was doing I would always keep one eye on them, even if I was chasing up and down having fun. They in turn, put a little bell on my collar next to my identity tag so they could hear me amidst all the trees and bushes.

At last I had all I could ever want: A safe, comfortable home, food and water, my very own family, a special little girl to love and I got to see my brother Charlie at least once a week.

My heart felt like a big ball of bread dough, packed with yeast and placed on a warm shelf to rise.

Chapter 17

Life with my forever family was just perfect and every day I counted my blessings. The memories of past hardships faded and were gradually replaced by new memories, made with my wonderful new family, for which I was eternally grateful. After a blissful few months in my forever home, Jenny was preparing the evening meal before Molly was due in from school, when the doorbell rang.

Toby and Otto barked of course, excited at the prospect of a visitor. Jenny dried her hands and went to the door. We could hear strange voices and shortly, a man and woman in uniform, came through to the kitchen diner. Jenny was in floods of tears and the woman was trying to comfort her.

'Is there anyone we can contact for you? Your husband perhaps, or another relative?'
'Yes, yes, my husband Bill.' Jenny sobbed. 'His number is in my phone.'

The man in uniform took her phone and called the number.

'Hello is that Mr Bill Willis? This is Sargent McDonald. I'm afraid there's been a road traffic accident outside school involving your little girl Molly. She is alive but quite badly injured I'm afraid and has been taken to the hospital. We're at your home with your wife… Yes, that's right, she's in Accident and Emergency. Can we all meet there in about half an hour?... Yes of course. See you there. Goodbye.'

Within five minutes everyone had left the house. At some point, the next door neighbour came around to feed us and let us out into the garden for a toilet break but it wasn't until much later that Jenny and Bill finally came home without Molly.

They both looked shattered and slumped onto the sofa as Bill hugged Jenny to him.

'Molly will pull through this. You heard what the doctor said. She's a little fighter, you'll see.'

The days dragged by interminably without her. I couldn't understand where my girl had gone and sat looking through the window all day, every day willing her to return. Jenny and Bill went to the hospital each day and when they returned I could detect Molly's scent on them but it was several weeks before I saw Molly again and I missed her terribly.

While she was away there was a lot of activity in the house; workmen coming and going, doing jobs around the house, making doorways wider and making adaptations to the bathroom and installing a special chair that went up and down the stairs at the push of a button.

Then, one day, Jenny and Bill arrived home after visiting Molly in hospital and I could sense their excitement. Balloons, buntings and banners were put up all around the house and lots of friends came around.

Molly was coming home!

When she arrived, I couldn't contain my excitement. I was the first in the queue to greet her, ecstatic and overjoyed, I did my signature bouncy, waggy tail, turning around in circles routine until I felt dizzy!

'Hector! Hector!' she exclaimed 'Have you missed me boy?'

There she was, the same beautiful girl with the same radiant smile but instead of standing up and walking towards me, she was sitting down in a chair with wheels on each side.

That didn't bother me one bit, she was still the same gorgeous child to me and I put my head on her little lap, looking up at her adoringly.

My girl was back where she belonged and my heart was restored.

Chapter 18

Life at home returned to normal once Molly was home and Otto, Toby and I still enjoyed our walks and plenty of hugs. I loved to sit next to her and followed her as she trundled around the house in her made to measure wheelchair. I sensed there was a new vulnerability about her which made me feel very protective.

After a few weeks, the relief of being back at home started to wear off and I could sense Molly becoming withdrawn and sad. She was sullen, irritable and infuriated that this limited way of life was all she had to look forward to.

'I'm just so angry mum. I'm trapped in this broken body, confined to this horrible wheelchair while that dreadful drunkard of a woman, who drove through a red light and knocked me down, is sentenced to one year in prison and then she'll walk free. Yes, mum! She'll walk! I'll never walk again and I'm stuck in this damn wheelchair for the rest of my life! Where's the justice in that mum…where?

I can't shower or dress by myself. I have to pee in a bag, can't control my own bowels! I can't do just normal basic stuff!
It's so humiliating having to rely on you and dad to do all that personal stuff for me. None of my friends want to know me anymore either.
I hate my life and I hate myself!'

I shared in her despair and put my head on her knee as Jenny tried to console her.

'Oh darling! It's true that it's not fair but unfortunately, life isn't always fair… but you know what? Sometimes the people who are dealt the worst cards are those who go on to win the game. It's about being positive. Think about what you can do rather than what you can't do. Your dad and me will be there to support you and we'll always love you whatever happens and whatever you do.'

But Molly was becoming more and more depressed. She refused to see anyone who came to visit her and would cry silent tears into my fur when we were alone, lying on her bed, in a warm doggy hug.

'Oh Hector, how am I ever going to lead a normal life? I might as well give up now. I wish that woman had killed me because this is a living death anyway. Others don't really care about disabled people. They pretend they do but they don't. Look at the number of people that park in disabled parking spaces when they're not disabled. Only yesterday mummy and me had to come home instead of going shopping because there was nowhere to park where I could get my wheelchair out of the car! Some selfish morons without blue badges had parked in the disabled spaces. Don't they realise it's illegal! I might as well just stay at home and rot!'

Molly had been away from school for a good while following the accident and when the prospect of returning loomed, she just refused to go and locked herself in her room.

Jenny and Bill tried hard to get her to do things; they planned lovely days out and started to even think about a holiday in Devon where Molly had always loved to go.

'How about it Molly, there's this fabulous cottage on the outskirts of Torquay, it's wheelchair and doggy friendly so we can all go as a family. We could all do with a change of scenery and a well-earned break. What do you think darling? It's available the week after next, it'll do you the power of good love.'

Molly just shrugged her shoulders, 'Yeh, Ok mum, I'm not that bothered but you're probably right.'

'Great!' Jenny enthused, giving Molly a hug. 'I'll book it online right now, I can almost smell the salty sea air already! Once you're there, you'll feel so much better, I just know it darling!'

Preparations for the holiday were in full swing and both Bill and Jenny were trying hard to maintain an atmosphere of positivity but a couple of days before we were due to go, Molly once more shut herself into her room and even locked me outside. She turned her TV up extra loud to drown out my pitiful whining, as I sat behind the door.

Eventually I gave up and just lay down, my head resting on my paws waiting patiently. But something wasn't right and after a while, something inexplicable alerted me. I just knew that all wasn't as it should be and started to whine and scratch at her door.

'Woof! Woof!' Let me in! I barked.

No response.

I barked again and again and scratched at Molly's door relentlessly but there was still no response. I needed to get help: I hurtled downstairs to Jenny who was busy packing up a box of supplies to take to the cottage.

'Woof! Woof!' I barked.

'What's the matter Hector, are you getting excited about the holiday too?'

No! I'm not! I thought. 'Woof! Woof!' I barked again and ran back upstairs to Molly's door and barked again and again. 'Woof! Woof!'

I scratched at the door frantically until Jenny appeared upstairs and knocked anxiously on the door.

'Molly? Are you ok? Molly? Answer me!' Jenny pushed at the door but it was locked fast. 'Molly! Open this door now Molly. You're upsetting Hector and worrying me!' But still there was no reply and the TV boomed.

Jenny ran downstairs in a panic and quickly returned with Bill.

'That's enough! We're going to break the lock Molly.' He shouted, trying to make himself heard over the TV.

'Molly, I'll count to ten. If you don't answer us by ten we're forcing the door, Ok? One, two, three, four, five, six, seven, eight, nine… ten!'
Bill pushed at the door, kicked it hard and eventually managed to break in. Molly was lying on the bed, her eyes shut and an empty bottle of tablets by her side.

I ran to her, jumped onto the bed and licked her sweet face.

'Oh Molly, Molly! Wake up, wake up!' Jenny shook her and Molly opened her eyes ever so slightly.

'What have you done Molly? Bill! What can we do? An ambulance might be too late. We need to take her to the hospital ourselves now!'
Molly's father gathered the limp body of his daughter in his arms and hurried downstairs. Jenny had already started the car up and they sped off down the road leaving Otto, Toby and me wondering what on earth had happened.

Later that day Molly's parents were back, without my girl. I went into the sitting room and looked through the front window, searching for a sign of Molly and wondering what was going on. Molly's parents were in there too and Jenny was sobbing.

'Oh God Bill! Her diary is just heart breaking. I know I shouldn't have read it but I was just so worried about her. To attempt suicide! She must be so desperately unhappy and I just don't know what to do to help her. After all the counselling following the accident, I thought she was starting to accept the situation but it's obvious that she isn't. It's so hard for her and it's so cruel.'

As Jenny cried, Bill put his arm around her and pulled her towards him.

'I've been thinking Jenny, you know how much Molly loves the dogs? Well, the other day, when I was in town, I saw a young woman in a wheelchair with a dog that was wearing a special coat saying: "Assistance Dog" on it, so…. I've been doing a bit of research.

The bad news is there's about a two-year waiting list to get a professionally trained assistance dog but the good news is, that there are a lot of people who have self-trained their own dogs to become assistance dogs and they can apply to become accredited through one of the official organizations. What do you think?'

'Well it's worth trying, isn't it? What do the assistance dogs do?' Jenny looked puzzled.

'Anything really, Guide Dogs for the Blind are the most obvious assistance dogs I suppose and Hearing Dogs for the Deaf of course but these days, dogs can be trained to help people with medical conditions such as diabetes and epilepsy as well as helping those with physical needs like Molly.

So, for instance these dogs can help with tasks like dressing, undressing, picking things up, opening doors, fetching things but, where I think it will really benefit Molly is with her reluctance to go to school, go out, mix with other people and so forth. Haven't you noticed how she's much more cheerful when the dogs are around? I think if she had a special dog dedicated to helping her, you know, one that could go everywhere she went, it might just help rebuild her self-confidence.'

Molly came home from hospital a few days later. Even though I was delighted to see her she ignored all my attempts to cheer her up. She seemed void of expression and just sat in her wheelchair blankly, in sullen silence. I pushed my nose under her hand, laid my head in her lap and tried to lick her face but she didn't respond.

The holiday had been cancelled and the house felt like some ominous black cloud was hanging over it.

'Molly?' Bill said. 'Molly, darling, mum and me have been talking about something which we think could help you.'

He went on to explain the idea of the special assistance dog and offered to get her a new puppy to train with the help of a one to one professional dog trainer.

'I don't mind trying it.' Molly said sulkily after a while.

'But, I don't need a puppy, I've got Hector and he's already my special dog.' She blurted.

'But Molly, love, Hector is a rescue dog from Cyprus. Yes, he's lovely but he's a scent hound; a hunting dog… You know how excited and driven he is when he's out on his walks, running around in the bushes chasing rabbits and squirrels. I think he'd really struggle with the discipline of training to do the specific tasks you need help with, I really do.' Jenny ventured.

'Then I won't do it.' Molly retorted.

'I want to give Hector the chance to do it mum. Remember what you said about those who are dealt the toughest hand can still win the game?
Well, I've done my research online and when I read about the dreadful things that happen to dogs like Hector in Cyprus well, it just makes my blood boil and makes it even more important that he's given a chance. He's had a terribly rough start but he's really clever too, I know he is, I see it in him every day mum, plus he knows me so well. Most of all, he's my best friend and I love him.'

I just watched on as Jenny and Bill capitulated and exchanged a glance with a resigned sigh.

'Ok Molly, you win.' Bill resolved.

'Tomorrow I'll contact that dog trainer who comes highly recommended and we'll ask him to come over and assess Hector's suitability for learning the things you need help with. How about that?'

Molly hesitated. 'Ok it's a deal. But I'm only agreeing because I know he'll pass the assessment with flying colours.'

I placed my paw on Molly's knee, looked up into her clear blue eyes and my heart was full of love.

Chapter 19

Within a few days, a dog trainer called Sam had visited the house. He was full of enthusiasm about the training:

'To be honest, with the right training most dogs can do the things you are suggesting.' He said. 'We see many breeds successfully complete the training. Hector is still young and eager to please, as well as being very food driven which are the main criteria. However, although I can't train him for you, I can show you how to train him yourselves. It will require perseverance, commitment and above all, perfect timing. Are you prepared for that?'

'Exactly what will it involve Sam? Can you explain how it works please?' asked Bill.

'Sure.' Sam replied. 'Perhaps the best way to explain it is to show you how it works. We find that the best method of training for these tasks is called clicker training. It's all about positive reinforcement. I'll show you how a very basic behaviour, for example, like Hector licking his lips, can be taught so that he does it on command.'

With that he called me over. He clicked the clicker and instantly gave me a treat. Very quickly, I understood that the sound of the clicker meant I was getting a reward. Great game!

Then, because I automatically licked my lips after eating the treat, he clicked again when I licked my lips and I got another treat! Better still! Sam then introduced the verbal command 'Lick!' As soon as I licked my lips, so I licked my lips again, got a click and another treat. I was enjoying this…what's not to love? Praise and food all at the same time!

'Wow, that's fantastic!' Jenny enthused.

Sam was emphatic though. 'It's all about getting the timing right. You must click at exactly the moment you see the action or behaviour who want to shape and encourage. It's also important that you only do the training for short bursts of time, so as not to overload the dog. It's imperative that Hector enjoys what he does. Do you want to give it a go Molly?'

Molly almost snatched the clicker from Sam. 'Silly question! Of course! Hector is my special boy and we're a team aren't we boy?'

And so, our training began. Sam still came to the house every week or two to check on our progress and introduce the next stage or discuss other tasks for me to try. We trained for just five minutes, twice a day and within a few weeks, I'd mastered picking up various objects in my mouth and placing them in Molly's lap. In a few months, I'd learned to help her undress, fetch different items she needed and would accompany her whenever we went out.

I also had a smart new red jacket with 'Assistance Dog in Training' written on it, which I wore every time we went out and about. It gave us access to a lot of public places that ordinary pet dogs weren't normally allowed to go to.

Although I wasn't yet fully trained and registered, the difference in Molly's demeanor and self-confidence was amazing. Molly's head teacher was so keen to encourage her back to lessons, that I was even given permission to accompany her into school. She resumed her education and started to rebuild her friendships with fellow pupils and my heart felt invigorated.

Chapter 20

Molly's confidence received a further boost a few weeks later with the arrival of a new electric wheelchair. She started to accept invitations to birthday parties and would meet her friends in the park on a Saturday morning and I would go too. It was a boost for us both. I was with Molly and she was with me and she blossomed into the girl she'd been before the accident. She even started using make up, buying new clothes and no longer avoided looking at herself in the mirror.

One summer evening, Molly and I were at home with her grandad. Jenny and Bill had gone out to celebrate their wedding anniversary, when Molly said,
'Fancy a nice little walk in the woods Hector?'
'Woof!' I replied. Do you need to ask?

'That's ok isn't it grandad? We won't be long.'

Grandad was, as usual, snoozing in the armchair and didn't respond straightaway.
She tried again a bit louder. 'Me and Hector are just going for a little walk down by the brook Grandad, it's such a lovely evening, we won't be long.'

Still half-asleep Grandad replied. 'Ok Molly, don't be long and don't forget to take your phone.'

Molly trundled down the garden path and through the back gate with me by her side. We followed the tarmacked footpath through the woods and down by the brook. Soon, I was doing my usual hunting dog act, sniffing around in the bushes and chasing anything that moved, one eye on Molly.

Suddenly my ears pricked up: An engine sound approaching from the distance. I'd never seen or heard any vehicles down by the brook before as it was just a footpath and there were no roads nearby. But, there was definitely something coming and the sound of the engine was getting closer and closer!

Not knowing if Molly had heard it too, I belted back towards her as fast as my legs would carry me, just in time to see the motorbike!

I barked a warning but the engine sound drowned me out and it hurtled around the sharp bend and smashed straight into Molly's wheelchair!

Molly screamed, her chair flipped onto its side, throwing her into the air and down the side of the bank towards the brook. The biker recovered quickly and jumped back onto the bike and with scant regard for Molly's welfare, rode off again, at great speed.

Molly! Molly! I raced down to where she lay. Her little body was all contorted and although conscious, she was dazed and had a nasty cut that oozed blood on her forehead. I licked her face willing her to speak to me.

'Hector, Hector,' she stuttered. 'Help me boy.' I grabbed hold of her little jacket to try and pull her up the bank but unfortunately, the jacket was made of such fine material that my teeth just ripped straight through it. Panic struck, I ran back up the bank and along the path looking for someone to help her but finding no one around, I hurried back to Molly's side.

'Hector, fetch phone boy, fetch phone.' She whispered.

I panicked in confusion. Fetch phone? That command was to bring Molly the landline phone at home when it rang. What should I do? I was at a loss, I just couldn't understand what she was asking of me!

Suddenly, I heard Molly's mobile phone ringing from the pocket of her upturned wheelchair. A phone! Instinctively, I dashed up the bank to the chair and desperately tried to get into the pocket to retrieve the phone but just as I managed to do it, the ringing stopped.

'Bring it Hector, fetch phone.' Molly called weakly. With great care, I picked up the mobile phone in my mouth and carried it delicately down the bank to Molly.

'Good boy Hector. Thank you.' She murmured.

With gargantuan effort, Molly managed to press something on her phone. 'Mum! It's me. I'm hurt, I'm down by the brook with Hector, please come quickly.'

With that, she passed out. All I could do was to lie by her side and bark and bay until my throat hurt.

Eventually, an elderly couple, out for a summer's evening stroll, heard my distress and called the emergency services. Molly's parents got there just as the paramedics arrived, who recovered Molly from the bank, placed her on a stretcher, carried her to the waiting ambulance and off to hospital, blue lights flashing.

Close to midnight, as I paced up and down with worry, Jenny and Bill came back. Jenny rushed straight up to me, hugging me so tightly I could barely breathe.

'Molly's going to be fine Hector, it's just mild concussion and she'll be home in a couple of days. You are a wonderful, brave boy and we'll never be able to repay your devotion to Molly. Thank you so, so much!'

I wagged my tail in delight and relief and my heart felt heroic!

Chapter 21

Sure enough, Molly came home as promised and, with her electric wheelchair repaired, she was soon back to her old self, chattering away, attending school and meeting up with her friends. A few weeks later when we arrived home from school, there was a letter waiting for her which she opened, a puzzled expression on her face.

'That's funny, no one ever writes letters to me, it's usually texts, messenger and emails these days.'

She read through the letter and looked at me and then her mum incredulously. 'What is it Molly?' Jenny asked.
'I can hardly believe it mum, look at this, look!' She said, excitedly holding out the letter to her mum.

'It's from an organisation called 'Lifelong Pals'. Hector has been nominated for the award of Best Rescue Dog of the Year!'
Jenny took the letter from Molly and scanned through it.

'Wow!' she exclaimed 'How fabulous! It says here that the award ceremony is being held at the Town Hall on the twelfth of next month. Hey! You'll need a new outfit Molly and Hector will definitely need a new collar and coat to wear! How exciting!'

The day of the award ceremony duly arrived and we all drove to the Town Hall. The place was teeming with people, dogs on leads and cats and rabbits in baskets. Members of the press were there, taking photographs and the sense of anticipation in the hall was palpable.

There were awards for dogs, cats and rabbits who had enriched people's lives in some way: Companion animals that visited the elderly or poorly people in homes, hospices and hospitals and assistance dogs who helped their owners with all manner of physical, medical and mental health issues.
There were also awards for animal heroes; those involved in law enforcement, wars and conflicts, who had saved soldiers, members of the police force and civilian lives.
The excitement was growing as Molly and I were called up onto the stage, with two other dogs and their owners.

The presenter of the awards, a man in a very smart grey suit, cleared his throat and paused.

'And now, it gives me great pleasure to announce the winner of the category of Rescue dog of the Year... Nominations are: Geoff Roberts with his dog Blue, Molly Willis with her dog Hector and Simon Bentley with his dog Luna.'
Loud applause ensued...... 'And the winner is...' The man opened the envelope and paused again.........

'Molly and Hector!' The place erupted.

I jumped up and down wagging my tail furiously, Molly's face beamed. Flash lights were going off everywhere as people took photos. It was amazing.

We moved forward to accept the certificate and trophy.

'May I say a few words to everyone please?' Molly whispered to the man. 'Of course.' He said, handing her the microphone as Molly passed him the trophy and certificate.

While she unfolded the piece of paper she'd had in her pocket, I put my paw up on to her knee. I adored this girl.

Hesitantly at first, she began:

'I hope you don't mind but with the help of my parents, I have prepared a short speech in case Hector was lucky enough to win this award, so here goes: Firstly, I would like to thank you for voting for Hector and thank the committee for organizing this fantastic event to celebrate these precious animals who are so much more than pets or working dogs.

Thank you to my family and friends who have supported me through the difficult times the tears and tantrums, but mostly, I have to say the biggest thank you to Hector... my amazing boy.'

Applause echoed around the huge hall. But Molly continued:

'Hector, if only he could speak, would be able to tell us of how he and other dogs like him, endure terrible hardship, starvation, barbaric cruelty and acute illness in a country where traditionally dogs aren't valued at all.
The prevalent attitude in Cyprus and in many other countries like Spain, Romania, Bulgaria and Serbia, not to mention the horrific treatment of dogs and cats in parts of South Asia, is that dogs and cats are disposable and of no moral value.

It is particularly harsh for hunting breeds like Hector who are regarded as "Just hounds."

These countries have no enforced animal welfare laws and dogs like Hector are lucky to survive passed the age of three or four, before being shot, hung to death, poisoned or abandoned to slowly starve and die.

Thankfully, there are a few wonderful people in these countries, who rescue and save as many dogs as they can and rehome them, often here in the UK and other European countries.
They give these dogs the chance to live full and active lives in loving homes.

When my family decided to rescue one of these dogs from Cyprus, little did we realise that Hector would actually come all the way from Cyprus to rescue me.
I owe him my life. He is my best friend, my helper, my soul mate, faithful companion and my world.

He is certainly not just a hound.

I dedicate this award to the thousands of dogs that suffer and die far too young, through cruelty and neglect. The poor dogs that never get the chance to show how special they can be as Hector has.

I also dedicate it to the marvellous people, who strive unstintingly to save as many dogs and cats as possible and campaign for better animal welfare laws in their countries' She paused.

'This award is really for them.'

The Town Hall erupted with whooping, loud whistles, cheers and clapping.

As I looked up into Molly's dewy eyes with love and pride, I wagged my tail and my heart sprouted wings and soared!

Post Script:

I'd been so lucky and enjoyed a full and wonderful life since coming to live with Molly and her family. Molly had regained her self-esteem and confidence, blossomed at school and grown into a beautiful, charming, funny and witty young woman with lots of friends and we were inseparable.

We'd also had some very exciting adventures together over the years and eventually, I'd gone to live with her at University where she'd achieved a degree and met her husband to be.

Now, at almost twelve years old, it was time for me to hang up my collar and lead and pass on the mantle of Molly's assistant, to another dog, even though I would carry on living with the family. Of the other family dogs, Otto had died the year before at the grand old age of sixteen and Toby was doing well and still his bossy, belligerent self, at nearly fourteen years old.

Molly contacted the dog rescue people in Cyprus, who found another abandoned hound for her to train and arrangements were made for it to travel to the UK.

The dog was a female and Molly named her Tia. She was a beautiful black and tan hunting dog, with the most stunning periwinkle blue eyes I'd ever seen, and my heart just melted.

Molly's Magic Wheelchair!

If you have enjoyed reading 'Just Another Hound' then you may like to read about Molly and Hector's fantasy adventures in 'Molly's Magic Wheelchair'.

Below are a couple of extracts to whet the appetite!

Chapter 2

Hector nudged Molly's hand and walked across the room and sat next to the new wheelchair which appeared to take over the best part of the dining room. Not that it was actually that big; it just seemed oversized and overstated because Molly wished it really wasn't there. Shortly after Hector had won the rescue dog of the year award two months before, a huge cardboard box had been delivered to the house and just left at the front door, addressed to Molly Willis and Hector the dog, England. That was it, no other address details, just Molly Willis and Hector the dog, England. Weird!

Intrigued, Molly's mum and dad had helped her open it to reveal this new shiny wheelchair and a scratchy hand-written note saying:

Please accept this as a token of my esteem.
Believe in it. Trust it. Use it wisely and use it for good. With best wishes B.B.

This cryptic message had quite unnerved Molly and she had shunned the new wheelchair: 'What do I need a new wheelchair for anyway?' She'd said to her parents. 'The one I've got already, is perfect for me, and not knowing where it's come from, well it's sort of strange and a bit, spooky!'

It wasn't as if they hadn't tried to find out where this mysterious gift had come from. They'd contacted the Post Office and all the other major delivery couriers to find out who'd delivered it, but drawn a blank.

None of the neighbours had seen it being delivered either. It was as if it had appeared out of nowhere, one minute it wasn't there, then the next moment it was: As if conjured out of thin air. Molly was dead against accepting the wheelchair and had wanted to return it to the sender or the shop from where is had come, but it had no return address and the maker's mark, '**MARVELLOUS MOBILITY INCORPORATED'** proved impossible to find: Company's House who register all UK businesses had no such business listed. So, the wheelchair was relegated to the corner of the dining room, like a misbehaving child sent to sit on the naughty step, and there it stayed gathering dust, instruction manual and all.

Today however, Molly was having to consider using it. Her old trusty electric wheelchair had developed a fault her dad hadn't been able to fix and had been taken to the repair workshop, where they'd said it would be a week before it would be ready. Molly had got an important presentation to give at a local primary school entitled: **Positively Disabled** and couldn't let them down. Her own school had encouraged Molly to accept the invitations that had followed the award Hector had won for 'Rescue Dog of the Year' as they knew it would help to improve her self-image and confidence.

Most of the children she spoke to were far more interested in meeting Hector than listening to Molly's talk. They just wanted to hear about his sad life in Cyprus before he'd been rescued and flown over to the UK and adopted by Molly and her family. They itched to hear about how he'd saved her life when she'd been so depressed following her accident that she'd attempted to commit suicide, and how he'd rescued her from yet another accident, when her wheelchair had been involved in a hit and run with a motorbike, illegally riding on a footpath. Yes, it was really Hector's exploits that really interested them.

Molly didn't mind, in fact she quite enjoyed this new-found celebrity status that Hector had acquired and for every presentation they did, a small donation was made to the charity training dogs for the disabled and the charity in Cyprus who had rescued Hector. Result!
Still, she thought, regarding the new wheelchair suspiciously, she didn't trust it one bit but using her old manual wheelchair, she knew that she'd never manage to do what she needed to do, so the new wheelchair, unfortunately, was her only option.

'Molly! Are you ready to go?' Called her mum. 'Dad's got an important meeting this morning, so if you want a lift to Greenway Primary you'll need to hurry up and get in to that new wheelchair!' Molly sighed and wheeled herself across the room and heaved herself out of her manual wheelchair and transferred herself into the strange new electric wheelchair. Settling herself into the seat she appraised the control panel on the arm of the chair.

Rather alarmingly, there were only two buttons. Go and Stop and a joy stick for direction. That's odd she thought. How will I be able to control the speed and where was the battery pack to power the chair? She hastily tore the plastic wrapping off the wheelchair manual and opened it. It was surprisingly brief and worse still, appeared to be in some strange Germanic language. Great! That's helpful, or not! She thought. Despite this and sensing that her dad was getting impatient to leave, she pressed go and guided the chair towards the front door, down the ramp, along the path and up the ramp into the back of the specially adapted van the family used to get about in. 'Come on Hector, work to do!' She called.

All seemed fine, the wheelchair had moved at just the right speed, she'd felt it slow down slightly as it went down the ramp and give a little power boost when it went up the steep ramp into the back of the van. She pressed stop. So far so good she thought, maybe it'll be alright after all. 'Believe in it. Trust it,' the scratchy note had said. Ok, so I'll just have to go with it then... well at least until I get my proper chair back next week, she thought as she clipped Hector's harness to the seat belt.

'Ready to go?' Her dad called, as he jumped into the driver's seat, belted up and started the engine.
'All present and correct captain!' Molly quipped. 'Woof!' barked Hector. He loved these special visits and seemed to sense when it wasn't an ordinary school day even before they'd loaded themselves into the van. He was such a clever boy. 'Good lad.' Molly patted his dark, noble head. 'Off we go!'

Chapter 15

Preeti helped Molly off her bed and into the wheelchair. 'What are we going to tell our parents about where we're going?' She asked.
'I don't know Preeti…. that's the least of our problems at the moment. However, I did notice something strange when I was with Bertie practicing with the wheelchair; when I got back, even though I thought I'd been gone all afternoon, only twenty minutes had passed here. Maybe time here passes more slowly than when I'm using the wheelchair's magic?'

'Well, let's hope so Moll, we'll just say we're going to the park with Hector and hope they don't miss us! Let's go! Got your magic manual?'

'Yep, got my head too!' Molly jested. 'Let's go and rescue Jacob. Come on Hector!' But before they were halfway to the door, the TV in Molly's room came to life and flickered, revealing the image of Bertie Baxter.
'Molly, it's Bertie. There's something I need to give you before you leave: The Amulets of Karinthia, which Wilfreda wants in exchange for Jacob's life.'

He'd decided not to divulge the truth about the fake amulets… he needed Molly to feel confident at all costs!

'Keep them secure and only hand them over when you know you are safe. 'I am sending them to you immediately by pigeon post. Look out for a stupid grey bird with a velvet pouch tied to its leg and leave a window open!' With that Bertie disappeared and the screen went black once more.

Preeti quickly opened the bedroom window but almost instantly, there was a loud splat against the other half of the window and a fat grey woodpigeon with a startled expression on its face, slid down the glass, top to bottom in slow motion, its wings outspread.

Preeti and Molly chuckled and Preeti leaned out and picked up the stunned bird, untying the pouch it was carrying, from its leg. The pigeon then came to, shook its head, wriggled out of Preeti's hands, pecked her thumb and flew off, narrowly missing a repeat performance with the inside of the window pane as it left!

Molly took the pouch and quickly looked inside. There they were, these jealously guarded and much coveted amulets. They resembled three mottled, yet shiny, golden egg-shaped jewels, each set in a silver surround with hieroglyphs symbols etched all around them.

Pulling the pouch strings closed she stuffed the pouch to the bottom of her jacket pocket.

Chapter 22

A Summons is Delivered

Bertie Baxter was in a real quandary:

He'd been summoned back to The Guild as a matter of urgency; a grizzle bat had arrived carrying a message written on dissolvable paper in invisible ink, tied to its leg.

The grizzle bat had been very bad tempered as she'd been woken up in the middle of the day to deliver the message so when she landed on Bertie's shoulder, she'd bitten his ear in annoyance! Of course, this made Bertie's ear bleed and this blood was now smeared on the note. However, once Bertie rinsed it with clean water, the message was still legible and explicitly clear.

'Bertram Baxter, return immediately to The Guild. A matter of extreme urgency has arisen.' Horatio Harbinger.

What did The Lord Chancellor want? Had they decided to banish him permanently? What was he to do about Molly and her wheelchair?

He clearly didn't have any choice and pronounced the spell to return him to The Guild to face his fate.

Find out what happens next and catch up with Molly, Hector and Bertie.

In

Molly's Magic Wheelchair!
By Suzanne Cadwallader

Due out July 2017

Printed in Poland
by Amazon Fulfillment
Poland Sp. z o.o., Wrocław